Management for the
XXI Century

Management for the XXI Century

Education and Development

The American Assembly
of Collegiate Schools of Business
and The European Foundation
for Management Development

Kluwer • Nijhoff Publishing
Boston/The Hague/London

DISTRIBUTORS FOR NORTH AMERICA:
Kluwer Boston, Inc.
190 Old Derby Street
Hingham, Massachusetts 02043, U.S.A.

DISTRIBUTORS OUTSIDE NORTH AMERICA:
Kluwer Academic Publishers Group
Distribution Centre
P.O. Box 322
3300 AH Dordrecht, The Netherlands

Library of Congress Cataloging in Publication Data

Main entry under title:
Management for the XXI century.

   1. Management — Congresses. 2. Industry — Social
aspects — Congresses. 3. Management — Study and
teaching — Congresses. I. American Assembly of
Collegiate Schools of Business. II. European
Foundation for Management Development. III. Title:
Management for the twenty-first century.

HD29.M316	658	81–23628
ISBN 0–89838–097–9		AACR2
ISBN 0–89838–098–7 (pbk.)		

Printed in the United States of America

Contents

Acknowledgments

The act of looking into the future requires considerable courage, some immunity from the taunts of skeptics, and, perhaps, a measure of innocence. To look into the future and assess its implications for management education and development is a task of even more formidable proportions. It is therefore with a deep sense of gratitude that the American Assembly of Collegiate Schools of Business (AACSB) and the European Foundation for Management Development (EFMD) recognize the contributions of the following members of the task force who designed and planned the three-phase project providing for such an assessment and who supervised the initial colloquium held at Windsor Castle, the follow-on colloquium at Arden House, and the international conference held in Paris:

Chairman: Luigi Dusmet, Partner
Consulting Partners/TASA, Zurich
Former dean, IMEDE, Lausanne

American members: William Voris, President
                      American Graduate School of Inter-
                         national Management
                      Glendale, Arizona

                      Boris Yavitz, Dean
                      Graduate School of Business, Colum-
                         bia University
                      New York

European members: Uwe Kitzinger, Dean
                      INSEAD
                      Fontainebleau

                      Mauk Mulder, Dean
                      Foundation for Business Administra-
                         tion
                      Delft

Secretary: Roger Talpaert, Secretary General
                      European Institute for Advanced Stud-
                         ies in Management
                      Brussels

Project director: Willem J. de Vries, Vice President,
                         EFMD
                      Former Deputy Group Personnel Co-
                         ordinator, Shell

EFMD representative: Jean-Francois Poncet,
                      Director General

AACSB representative: Robert H. B. Wade, Director
                      Washington Office

The project owes much to the vision and leadership of Arnoud
W. J. Caron, president of EFMD from 1974 to 1980. In addition,
special recognition is given to Jacques Lesourne, chairman of the
Windsor Castle colloquium; Boris Yavitz, chairman of the Arden
House colloquium; and Vernon K. Zimmerman and Grigor Mc-
Clelland, co-chairmen of the Paris conference. Special recognition
is also given to Clarence C. Walton, who served as synthesizer at the
Arden House colloquium and the Paris conference and editor of the
reports of both meetings; to Maurice Saias, who also served as synthesizer of the Paris conference; and to James Robertson, who served
as editor of the Windsor Castle report. Thanks also to William K.

Laidlaw, Jr., and Michael N. Staniforth, who served as members of the organizing committee of the Paris conference; and to the many others who contributed to the success of the AACSB/EFMD project.

We wish also to thank the following organizations for their support of the two colloquia and the international conference:

United States:

Arthur Andersen & Co. Foundation
Association of MBA Executives
General Electric Foundation
Monsanto Fund
Peat, Marwick, Mitchell and Co.
Richard D. Irwin Foundation
Touche, Ross & Co.
TRW Foundation
U.S. Department of State

Europe:

Bos Kalis Westminster Group (NL/UK)
Fondation Industrie-Université (B)
Fondation Nationale pour l'Enseignement de la Gestion des Entreprises (F)
Foundation for Management Education (UK)
Friesch-Groningsche Hypotheekbank (NL)
Heineken Brouwerijen (NL)
Hollandse Beton Groep (NL)
IBM Europe (F)
IBM Belgium (B)
Internatio Muller (NL)
Koninklijke Distill. Erven Lucas Bols (NL)
Nationale Nederlanden (NL)
Norit (NL)
Philips Gloeilampenfabriek (NL)
Royal Dutch/Shell Group (UK/NL)
Social Science Research Council (UK)
Unilever (NL)
Van Ommeren (NL)
Vroom and Dreesmann (NL)

The project, involving close and fruitful collaboration between management educators and managers on both sides of the Atlantic, will, we believe, make a significant and lasting contribution to the future of management education.

EFMD BOARD OF TRUSTEES
AACSB BOARD OF DIRECTORS

An Introduction to the Project

Paris in springtime is the fabled city of a fabled season. This fascinating place and enchanting time were the setting for a June 15–18, 1980 conference on management education, the final phase of a historic cooperative effort between Americans and Europeans, the culmination of three years' work on an exciting project entitled "Management and Management Education in a World of Changing Expectations."

The project involved a look ahead at the thirty-year period from 1980 to 2010, the changes likely to occur during that time, and the implications for management and management education. Sponsored by the American Assembly of Collegiate Schools of Business (AACSB) and the European Foundation for Management Development (EFMD), it had two stages prior to the Paris conference — the first, a futures-oriented colloquium held in February 1979 at St. George's House, Windsor Castle, on "The Changing Expectations of Society"; the second, a colloquium held in November 1979 at Arden House, Columbia University, on "Management for the XXI Century." The theme of the Paris conference was "Managers for the XXI Century: Their Education and Development." While sponsored by AACSB and EFMD, the Paris conference was actually a worldwide meeting, with corporate leaders and deans or directors of business schools throughout the world invited to participate. Representation came from all continents, with 650 participants from thirty-five countries.

What is special about the joint project is not that it was the first international effort of deans of business schools and corporate leaders interested in management education, important as that might be. What is of more significance is that it represented an attempt on the part of management schools to face up to the challenges of the future and see what might be done to meet them. It was all the more remarkable in that this effort for reform was brought about, not in the normal pattern by some external force or outside initiative, but by a recognition of the need for self-examination and self-renewal, the momentum arising from within management education itself. What is also notable is that the reform was not sparked by the work of a few scholars, as in the case of the Gordon/Howell and Pearson reports of the late 1950s, both of which had a significant influence on management education by setting standards of scientific and professional attainment. Instead, the Paris conference and its earlier, preparatory stages involved the work of literally thousands of academics — deans and faculty — and top-level practitioners from the world of business, working together to draw up a road map for the future of management education.

Genesis of the Project

The project had its genesis in the realization by the leaders of both organizations, AACSB and EFMD, that there are at work in the world today forces producing both rapid change and changing expectations. In the developed countries this change is of a sociopolitical nature and involves such trends as the shift from goods to services and the public-private dichotomy. In the developing countries the change generally aims at higher levels of employment and a rise in the general standard of living and involves such trends as the transfer of technology and the development of human resources.

It was felt that management on both sides of the Atlantic would want to anticipate these changes and that management education would also want to take account of them in order to train competent and effective managers for the XXI century. A thirty-year time frame was selected because the project planners felt it represented the crucial joining of an old and a new millennium. More practically, the rationale for the time horizon of thirty years was that those who will be senior executives of major corporations and organizations in the year 2000 have already graduated from our institutions. Hence, if the project was to influence the future executive, it had to look beyond the year 2000.

Windsor and Arden House Colloquia

The Windor colloquium had agreed that, in thinking about the future, there were eight fundamental questions or issues that merited attention:

- The availability of resources, especially nonrenewable sources;
- The changing international order, as East-West relations are influenced in dramatic ways by North-South relations;
- The changing values in postindustrial society;
- Disenchantment with institutions in society — government, corporations, and trade unions;
- Increasing obligations to classes and special groups — women, youth, senior citizens, and minorities;
- The importance of science and technology (e.g., to production);
- The vulnerability of complex societies to terrorism and other kinds of threats;
- The need for a holistic approach to issues and actions.

At Arden House, three major themes were addressed:

- The legitimacy and authority of management and the governance of organizations;
- The changing functions and roles of managers;

- The motivation, satisfaction, and morale of managers.

Published reports of both colloquia had been made available to the Paris conferees. In addition, two papers provided a backdrop for the conference — one, a report from the AACSB annual meeting, held the previous week in Chicago, which discussed the same theme; the other, a parallel input from EFMD based on national papers and on a January 1980 Oslo meeting of directors of schools.

A Participatory Conference

The Paris conference opened with two keynote addresses — one by a prominent American industrialist, William P. Tavoulareas, president of Mobil Corporation; and the other by a distinguished French statesman, Jacques Chaban-Delmas, president of the French Assemblée Nationale and a former prime minister of France. Reflecting the action-oriented man of business, Mr. Tavoulareas spoke of the twin dangers of overconfidence in long-range planning and of the subtle parochialism that occurs when one nation attempts to impose its legal obligations on multinational corporations operating under other nations' laws and in different cultures. Consequently, he felt, a prime requirement of educators is that they stress flexibility as the essential quality of managers in the future. Mr. Chaban-Delmas, taking a more philosophical stance, emphasized the importance of free initiatives by political and business leaders if human dignity is to be preserved and enhanced in a turbulent world. Managers, he pointed out, will have to reconcile the demands of competitive success with human needs for freedom and dignity; and they will be expected to respond not simply to imperatives of efficiency but to demands for equity as well.

A distinguishing feature of the Paris conference was its organization and dynamics. It was, in every sense of the word, a *working* conference that generated excitement and enthusiasm as it moved along. It was organized around the following three themes:

- Managers of the future (a theme intended to provide a link to and continuity with Arden House);
- Challenging issues facing management education and development in the next thirty years;
- Institutional responses: programs for action.

The participatory nature of the conference, which contributed greatly to its outcome, was evident in the manner in which conferees committed themselves to the intellectual analysis and distillation process and to the formulation of the major recommendations and conclusions. Their attendance at the rapidly succeeding working sessions and their adherence to the demanding schedule of the conference were evidence that interest and motivation, as well as creativity and spontaneity, were sustained throughout. In a real sense, the delegates were shareholders in the conference.

The Challenge

There was nothing about the two colloquia or the Paris conference that was "managed" or preordained, and yet their highlights and conclusions represent a striking convergence of views on both sides of the Atlantic, with differences expressed mainly in the form of nuances rather than strongly held dissents. Its organizers believe the project represents a kind of watershed event that attained and even surpassed established goals while strengthening the ties that bind the members of the two associations, individually and collectively.

All involved in the three-year project realize, nevertheless, that much remains to be done. Ideas and recommendations for the future need to be given practical expression; they need to be further evaluated and implemented. This will be the challenge! If the means can be found to do what needs to be done, there can be a creative and imaginative renewal in management education, a renewal such as was experienced twenty years ago when the Carnegie Corporation and Ford Foundation initiatives resulted in the publication of the Gordon/Howell and Pearson reports. If the AACSB/EFMD project can be the catalyst, the spark plug, for such a revival, it will have contributed significantly to the future of management education and will have achieved the primary purpose of its planners.

* * *

The volume that follows has three parts, each the product of one of the three meetings referred to above. Reports on these meetings have been published separately. They are brought together here for the first time in a single volume.

PART I

Societal Expectations and Trends, 1980–2010

CHAPTER 1

The Changing Expectations of Society in the Next Thirty Years

JAMES ROBERTSON

This opening chapter summarizes the main points that arose in the discussions at the Windsor Castle colloquium. It makes no attempt to summarize or discuss the various papers presented at that time. Instead, it brings into broad perspective the issues and questions that arose in the course of the meetings and that are the subject of this volume.

The chapter is structured as follows: The first part deals with the basic societal issues likely to confront management over the next thirty years. Next, further questions are raised concerning the challenges management will face in the future. Finally, the last part of the chapter is devoted to the responses of management to these challenges, as well as the implications of the challenges for management development, management education, and education in general.

Some Underlying Questions

TIME HORIZON

Assuming that the AACSB/EFMD project is successful, it will result in changes in management education/development. These changes will begin to take effect in the early to middle 1980s and will contribute to the education of students of management from that time on. Many of those students may expect to achieve positions of influence in the following twenty to twenty-five years. This line of reasoning suggests, therefore, that a time horizon of about thirty years is both appropriate and necessary. How meaningful is it to discuss today the management implications of possibilities as distant in time as that?

PERSPECTIVE

Our perspective is primarily that of contemporary management in the industrialized countries of Europe and North America. But even within those countries today, different conditions and different needs loom large in different places, and different people hold widely different perspectives. As we look into the future and beyond Europe and North America, the range of differing perspectives grows even wider. Over the next thirty years managers will, in fact, increasingly find themselves operating in a plurality of conditions, perspectives, and cultures. Even if they try to retain the outlook of the managerial classes in industrialized countries today, they will need to understand the different priorities and different values of different peoples in a multicultural world. How far will they find it possible to do this without altering their own perspective, and thus adopting a perspective significantly different from ours?

UNCERTAINTY

The most certain thing about the next thirty years is that they will be full of uncertainty. Resource availability and scarcity, the aspirations of people, geopolitical developments — on these and other vital aspects of the future, experts and laymen alike disagree deeply. Living with uncertainty is likely to be management's biggest challenge. This will demand great flexibility. Is that a practical demand to present to management today (even if only for discussion), environed as today's management is by the rigidities shown by many large business organizations (there are some striking and dramatic expectations of nonrigidity among those organizations!), by governments, by big trade unions, and by all the pressure groups of modern industrial society?

CHANGING DEFINITIONS

What is management? Twenty years ago most people probably took it to refer to the management of profit-making businesses. Today many people, especially in Europe, would extend it to include the management of nationalized industries and other public sector corporations, the management of public services such as education and health, the management of religious institutions, and the management of trade unions. It is possible that the prevailing definition of management may in future be extended further to include the management of "alternative" enterprises and associations, such as self-built housing cooperatives, common ownerships, local amenity enterprises, work experience projects, and so forth. In that case, the concepts of social invention, social innovation, and the social entrepreneur will play a significant part in management education and development. But how far can these concepts be given practical meaning in the context of management today?

CHANGING VALUES

It is not only the people with whom managers have to deal whose values will change. The values of managers themselves may change. For example, a new criterion of management success may emerge in place of growth (although it has to be acknowledged that, even today, growth is no longer the sole criterion). In thirty years successful management may perhaps be management that, within the constraint of economic viability, contributes effectively to the personal and social development of the people and communities with whom it deals. Or again, the distinction between managers and those managed may become less clear. How can possibilities of that kind be usefully discussed today? What practical implications can they be given in the context of management as it now is?

CONFLICTING VISIONS OF THE FUTURE

In this volume Daniel Bell (and, to some extent, Jan Tinbergen also) presents a vision of "postindustrial society" in which the dominant factors would include the expansion of science-based industries, professional services and research, the centrality of theoretical knowledge as the source of economic innovation and as the basis for formulating policy questions, and the management of complexity. Ignacy Sachs, on the other hand, presents a vision of "decentralized ecodevelopment" that would liberate people from domination by megabureaucracies, technostructures, and megamachines. Daniel Bell's vision implies the consolidation, and even the acceleration, of many of the dominant trends in late industrial societies, whereas Ignacy Sachs' vision implies a discontinuity or change of direction away from those trends and a search for "transition strategies from maldevelopment to genuine development."

Which of these visions of the future should be adopted? The future is likely to be shaped (at least in part) by continuing tension and conflict between forces making for a more technocratic, professionalized society and forces making for a more self-reliant, people-centered society. Should managers today and in the future be on one side or the other? Or should they, rather, remember the saying: If you want to stay in the circus, you must learn to ride two horses at once.

DIFFERENT WAYS OF STRUCTURING
THE DISCUSSION

The structure of discussion adopted here is, broadly, as follows:

- What are the challenges to management?

- What is the management response?
- What are the implications for education?

But the discussion could be structured in a variety of ways. For example:

- What will people want in the future?
- What factors will constrain the scope for meeting these wants?
- What situation will result?
- How should management respond?
- What sort of education will management need?

Again, it would be equally possible to ask:

- What constraints will affect the continuation of current trends?
- How will these constraints affect people's wants?
- What situation will result?

Alternatively, if one starts from an analysis of management tasks, then all the issues raised could best be looked upon as different aspects of two basic dimensions of managerial action:

- The economic, rational dimension;
- The political, nonrational dimension.

In this view the future depends on the dynamic interaction between these two basic dimensions of managerial action.

If too rigidly adopted, any structure will limit or distort the course of discussion. The answers reached will be determined, at least to some extent, by what questions are chosen.

SUMMARY

All the points noted above — time horizon, perspective, uncertainty, changing definitions, changing values, the opposition between conflicting visions of the future, and the possibility of structuring discussion in various ways — seem to emphasize the increasing importance for management of the need, as Abraham Maslow put it, "to tolerate the simultaneous existence and perception of inconsistencies, oppositions, and flat contradictions." That may be a useful frame of mind in which to approach the issues discussed in the next section.

Some Challenges to Management

The main questions raised in this section are summarized under the following seven headings:

- Availability and scarcity of resources;
- The changing international order;
- Changing values in postindustrial society;
- Institutions in society;
- Classes and groups of people;
- Science, technology, and production;
- The vulnerability of complex societies and the need for a holistic, interdisciplinary approach.

AVAILABILITY AND SCARCITY OF RESOURCES

What general attitude should management take? At least three attitudes are to be found among the general public today:

- *Doomsday:* Everything is being depleted and polluted at an ever-accelerating rate; ecological disaster impends.
- *No problem:* Technical ingenuity and the price mechanism, working together through the normal interactions of supply and demand, can be relied on to provide substitutes and solutions as the need arises.
- *Constructive realism:* Ecological prudence and sensible planning can help us to evolve more effective resource strategies ahead of time.

Which of these will be the most appropriate attitude for managers? Will different attitudes be appropriate to different circumstances?

Work on alternative sources of energy and materials (and on the substitution of available forms for scarce forms of energy and materials) will grow in importance.

What business opportunities and threats will this stimulate? What government strategies will it imply? What time constraints will be relevant? As conventional sources of energy and materials are depleted, the capital costs of some new energy sources (including research and development costs) will be much higher than those of the conventional sources. May this imply that further investment will become uncommercial for corporate financing? At what point would it become uneconomical even for governments to finance? Is there any serious prospect of a worldwide capital shortage?

Can we have an economically growing society that uses less energy and resources? Will conservation generate new business opportunities? Will the management of conservation be a future growth point? Could successful management of, for example, the energy industries involve helping customers to make better use of *less* energy? What new ways of measuring successful management performance would this imply? What trade-offs will people make between levels of consumption (of energy and other resources) and the following:

- Rising prices;
- Pollution or loss of amenities;
- Risk of catastrophe (e.g., from nuclear power);
- Undesirable working conditions (e.g., in coal mines).

Furthermore, as values shift, how may the trade-offs change?

Many countries will find themselves increasingly dependent on imports of energy and other scarce resources.

Will their greater dependence and vulnerability in this respect mean that new national strategies will be adopted for securing supplies? Such strategies might include (1) a proliferation of bilateral agreements, or (2) more aggressive foreign policies.

May greater national dependence and vulnerability in the sphere of resources also lead to risk-avoidance strategies? Could these involve a move towards economic structures and arrangements that are more robust, even if less productive in conventional terms? To what extent would more robust economic structures be more decentralized and self-sufficient? To what extent would they involve a revival of informal economic activity? And what are the implications of all this to the manager (of either private or public organizations), not simply to the policy-maker or government leader?

THE CHANGING INTERNATIONAL ORDER

For nearly thirty years, from the end of World War II until 1973, the noncommunist world's approach to international economic relations was based on an approximation to free trade. That era now seems to be over. (An era also appears to have ended for the communist nations, although the process went in an opposite direction.)

What will take the place of the era of free trade? Will any viable new system of international economic interdependence emerge in the next thirty years?

There is a wide economic/material gap between the rich countries of the North and the poor countries of the South.

Will this gap widen? Or will the rising prices of commodities (e.g., oil) and the increasing number of middle-income countries help to bridge the gap? May world development strategies emerge that positively encourage lower levels of consumption in the richer countries as well as higher levels in the poor ones? And will they prove acceptable/implementable to the public and governments alike?

Trade between North and South may face a structural crisis. Slower growth in the North may reduce its demand for imports from the South, and higher unemployment could lead to protectionist barriers.

In this situation, how far will common interests be able to pull the poor countries together? How far will they be also able to sink their differences in order to insist on new rules for the international trading game?

Meanwhile, trade between industrialized countries may also suffer from low growth and high unemployment.

How far will those countries be able to achieve a common position vis-à-vis the developing countries? How far will they find it necessary to erect further protectionist barriers against one another?

Although the North-South relationship is prominently mentioned above, the East-West confrontation will continue to be one of the realities of life.

It has been suggested that in the year 2000 the United States could have a 10 percent share in world GNP, compared with a 32 percent share in 1970. More generally, the countries of North America and Western Europe could see their shares of the world GNP decline from around 60 percent in 1970 to 32 percent in the year 2000.

How far will the geopolitical balance of economic power swing in favor of energy-exporting, resource-exporting, food-exporting countries as opposed to technology-exporting countries?

Bilateral agreements between individual countries (or trading blocs like the European Community) may become an increasingly important feature of the international economy.

What prospect is there of the emergence of a world authority capable of enforcing bilateral agreements? What signs are there at present that, in this or any other way, a stable new framework for international economic relations or a clear new direction for world economic development is likely to take shape?

What does this uncertain future hold for transnational corporations (TNCs)? On the one hand, they can move money, people, materials, technology, and know-how across national boundaries, thus creating flexibility in a world where 150 national governments exercise local sovereignty. On the other hand, they are seen as unaccountably, even irresponsibly, free of regulation and control by governments. They have a unique capability to contribute to a country's development, and host countries go out of their way to attract them. At the same time they are accused of exploiting Third World peoples, distorting their economies, and creating new dimensions of dependency. They have been identified with the conventional "trickle down" approach to development. If the pendulum is now beginning to swing in favor of indigenous self-development from the bottom up, what will that mean for the TNCs?

The doubts and contradictions mentioned above probably mean that TNCs should expect to receive increasingly inconsistent treatment from governments in industrialized and Third World countries alike. They may also find it more and more difficult to reach satisfactory long-term agreements with governments in all countries, especially since the expected life of governments is so much shorter than that of TNCs.

In this context the internationalization trend of the (European) trade unions should be mentioned. What prospect is there that new international institutions will evolve to regulate relations between TNCs and national governments? What form might such institutions take? Wise and effective supragovernmental regulation of the TNCs might be welcomed by them if it also provided them with some protection (at the same time) from arbitrary actions (such as confiscatory expropriation, unfair taxation, and the like) by the government of the host country.

CHANGING VALUES IN POSTINDUSTRIAL SOCIETY

A general shift of emphasis has been apparent in some sectors of the population in industrialized countries in recent years — a shift away from largely material and economic goals towards social and personal goals.

This emphasis on quality of life is likely to continue. At the same time the demand for higher levels of material well-being, more jobs, et cetera, may also continue to strengthen. It may be many years before this apparent contradiction is resolved. People, of course, being people, want both.

There is likely to be increasing diversity in the values and aspirations held by different persons, different groups, and different countries.

This is partly because modern communications show people that many alternative ways of life are possible, in contrast to the single prevailing set of standards offered by a closed society. Increasing diversity is partly due, also, to different cultural norms that will continue to affect behavior in different countries — for example, career advancement through job mobility will probably continue to be more prevalent in the United States than in Europe.

A final cause of diverse values is the fact that the balance between material and nonmaterial needs is different for different persons and different countries.

In this situation of shifting and diverse values, how can management best equip itself to keep the right balance between economic and social factors and to tailor its approach to the particular set of values, aspirations, and priorities of the people and societies with whom it has to deal?

The demand for flexibility and variability in personal life is likely to grow.

This will affect the various groups of people with whom managers deal. It will also affect managers themselves. People will want to be able to move between situations; between work, studies, and leisure; between different kinds of jobs and between different lifestyles. They will also demand much greater flexibility in how they do their jobs. Personal self-discovery and self-development will be a central project for many people, and the organization for which they work will be regarded as an instrument for that purpose.

Will a consequence of these trends be that employees will come to feel less and less attached to the organization for which they work? Should corporations set out to fulfill their employees' personal needs as well as their economic needs, and at what price?

The demand is also likely to grow for more genuine participation in corporate and societal decision-making. It will become increasingly difficult to get things done by appeal to hierarchical superiority, tradition, or even expertise. Many people will want to have a say in decisions and to feel that their opinions are taken seriously (for others the demand for participation may to some extent be symbolic only, and when given the opportunity to participate, they may opt not to).

This is likely to reinforce other pressures making for decentralization and for smaller organizations that allow for more direct personal involvement and influence. Does this mean that conventional forms of company ownership and control may increasingly be questioned? May we even see the emergence of a new form of organization that is little more than a confederation, or even a temporary coalition, of self-employed entrepreneurial groups?

The demand for flexibility in personal life and participation in social decision-making will be linked for many people with the search for a new sense of meaning and stability. These people will want to feel that they are living socially productive, personally fulfilling lives, better integrated than many people's lives today. They will look for ways of relating the use they make of their working time with the use they make of their free time. Voluntary simplicity and the desire to live in closer harmony with nature may become more widespread.

What proportion of the population is likely to be affected in these ways? How deeply? And will these trends be reversed if material well-being is threatened by long periods of low growth and high unemployment?

These conflicting possibilities may be especially significant in the context of work. On the one hand, there are many signs of a growing concern with work as a source of creative fulfillment, not just as a source of income. This may prompt increasing numbers of people to seek self-defined work in conditions of self-employment and to throw aside those aspects of the puritan work ethic that have hitherto encouraged people to seek jobs. On the other hand, continuing high unemployment may prompt people to compete for scarce jobs with renewed commitment. Both these things may happen. Some people may move in the first direction, others in the second. But which is likely to be the dominant trend?

Unless conditions arise in which many people find that survival has become the overriding goal, it seems likely that concern will continue to grow for the environment, for equality (at least of treatment and opportunity), and for human rights and the rights of future generations.

This will add new dimensions to the concept of corporate social responsibility and to the problem of corporate legitimacy. In order to maintain legitimacy, corporations may increasingly have to show that they are performing socially as well as economically useful functions. Linked with this are the changes now taking place in the structure of many power relationships: workers/management, women/men, South/North, East/West. It can be argued that change in power relationships, in factual strivings and behaviors, is in fact at the root of changing values: People find ways of reducing these power differences and consequently also change their expressed values, opinions, et cetera. This change in factual power differences within corporations, churches, trade unions, and the like is connected with, among other things, the information technology (r)evolution. How best will management be able to come to terms with these shifting concepts of responsibility and these shifting balances of power?

INSTITUTIONS IN SOCIETY

Many changes may be expected to take place in the next thirty years in the goals and structures of institutions such as governments, business corporations, and trade unions, and in the structure of relationships between them.

These changes will occur partly under pressure to make the institutions more responsive to the changing balances of power they are expected to transform into societal action, and partly because — as power relationships continue to shift — people in the various institutions will seize new openings and opportunities to improve their position. But changes will also take place in the relationship between people and institutions generally. The claims of all institutions may come to be regarded with increasing skepticism. They may come to be perceived as blocking, rather than facilitating, the transformation of social values into societal action. This will be a challenge to the very context in which managers work. How will management best prepare to meet it?

Relations between the so-called public and the so-called private sector are likely to change in various ways. Governments will be under pressure to involve themselves more closely in industry and the economy — for example, to control inflation and unemployment. At the same time governments' previous lack of success in this field has already led to considerable public disenchantment with government intervention and regulation, and this is likely to grow.

How will this apparent contradiction work itself out? May we see an increasing demand for forms of government intervention and regulation that will encourage decentralized self-regulation of a socially productive kind? What forms of intervention and regulation would these be? What would they imply for management? And how could management help to formulate them?

Similar questions arise about the future role of trade unions. It is generally recognized that the employee interest should be represented in industrial and economic decision-making and that it will have to be more effectively represented in the future than in the past if solutions to economic and industrial problems are to be found. But at the same time there is widespread disenchantment with what is perceived as the irresponsible power of the trade unions and their backward-looking approach.

How is the participation of the members within trade unions factually operating? How will these apparent contradictions work themselves out?

Important differences exist between the United States and Europe as regards the public/private dichotomy. In the United States there are virtually no publicly owned enterprises and there is virtually no concern among trade unions for codetermination or self-management. There is a growing public wish that private corporations should adopt social goals and a growing readiness on the part of corporations to take the appropriate initiatives. In Europe, on the other hand, many countries have an important range of publicly owned enterprises; trade unions are a strong political force; the scope and size of the public sector is a question for continuing political debate; industrial strategy and corporate responsibilities are an issue in the politics of Left versus Right; and corporations (in comparison with their U.S. counterparts) feel they have comparatively little scope for initiative as regards their social responsibilities. However, in one respect at least, convergence between the United States and Europe is apparent. While the large U.S. private corporation has been taking on a wider and wider range of social obligations, the European state-owned enterprise has been under increasing pressure to meet commercial criteria in its day-to-day operations. In Europe governments are intervening in the life of private corporations on a wide scale by financing in various ways the corporations' losses (shipyards, machine industry, textile industry). In the United States corporations are indirectly supported by restrictive government measures — for example, American civil servants have to use American carriers, and dredging work can only be done with dredgers and other material produced in the United States. As the need to pursue both economic and social goals continues to be increasingly recognized on both continents, what other examples of convergence may we expect in their socioeconomic structures? What general implications may this have for the roles of the state and the market?

The politicization of economic life may make it increasingly difficult to secure the necessary support of disparate groups for major decisions.

We can already see increasingly frequent deadlock between competing groups (such as power workers, transport workers, computer operators, medical personnel, and various professional groups), many of whom have the ability to block or disrupt the activities of complex modern societies. As more and more people, interest groups, pressure groups, and lobbies get into the game, will its growing complexity create a severe crisis in the ability of the political system to make choices and decisions? If this happens, how shall we attempt to resolve conflicts between the good of particular groups and the good of society as a whole? Shall we find ourselves driven to more authoritarian forms of government? One must have reservations about the feasibility, as well as the desirability, of that course. Shall we simply find ourselves, as the overload on central political authorities becomes more and more acute, relying *faute de mieux* on ad hoc forms of decentralized decision-making to muddle through?

Big business, as well as government and trade unions, is also the object of a certain public disenchantment. Large corporations are perceived to have disadvantages and small businesses to have advantages, including the ability to create more jobs relatively. Research on mergers in Europe indicates that many of the bigger, merged companies do worse than was anticipated — worse than the sum of the component companies has done and would have done. Small companies appear to be responsible for a "disproportionately large proportion" of the important innovations. Does this mean we may expect a marked revival of small businesses and entrepreneurial activity in a greatly decentralized economy? Will this lead to new demands for venture capital? Will venture capital be available? From what sources? May a revival of decentralized economic activity merge with the growing emphasis on the social functions of business to create an increasing role for small, nonprofit organizations whose aim will be to help make the social and environmental quality of life financially self-supporting? What implications could this have for management? And for finance?

Industrialized societies may be suffering from an increasing rigidity of institutional response, which could get worse.

How many people in institutional situations — in government, business corporations, public services, professions — are already finding that they have less and less room for maneuver and less and less scope for initiative? Is there already a widespread feeling that, when we make changes in institutional structures and procedures to meet today's demands, we often only make tomorrow's problems worse? What does this imply for business, government, and the economy? And what will be the appropriate management response?

CLASSES AND GROUPS OF PEOPLE

The role of the family, and the roles and relationships of men, women, young people, and old people, will continue to change. Minority groups, such as the handicapped, will probably claim their rights more vigorously than in the past. Most societies are likely to have to come to terms with a plurality of ethnic groups that also claim their rights more vigorously.

All this could have profound implications for economic activity and for management during the next thirty years. In the United States recent surveys have shown that over 50 percent of families now have a working wife, and 60 percent of all new jobs have been going to women. Meanwhile, the importance of the conventional family (mother, father, children) continues to decline. One recent study showed that 23 percent of households were single-parent families. However, in spite of these changes, traditional attitudes remain widespread (e.g., men's work is typically paid work outside the home, and women's work is typically unpaid work for the family in the home). Two contradictory trends thus seem possible in the next few years. On the one hand, will the increasing demand for flexibility in life and work, combined with continuing pressure for equality of career opportunity for women, lead to a more equal distribution of both paid and unpaid work between men and women? On the other hand, will low growth and high unemployment create pressures on women to go back into the home and leave the scarce paid jobs to men? Which of these trends is likely to be the stronger? How may they interact? What may they mean for management?

Increasing numbers of young people now have access to some form of higher education. At the same time there is evidence that increasing numbers of young people, whether or not they reach the university level, are questioning the relevance of the education they are offered. Increasing numbers of young people are facing the prospect of unemployment when they leave school and are finding it difficult to define a satisfactory social role and personal identity for themselves as adults.

If more flexible patterns of work and life become a general norm, some of these problems may be eased. But if low growth and high unemployment result in more rigid discrimination between those who are employed and those who are not, the problems may become more acute. The position and prospects of young people are now raising deeply important questions for the future of industrialized societies. How can management best equip itself to address these questions?

Demographic changes in industrialized societies mean that the population is becoming more elderly. The voice of senior citizens is beginning to be heard more loudly. There are conflicting trends toward earlier and later retirement.

Will these result in the elderly claiming the right both to work and to receive a pension? Will they intensify the competition for scarce jobs and increase the pressures on overstretched public expenditure? Or will they combine with the trend toward more flexible patterns of life and work to give an acceptable choice between early and late retirement?

The growing international character of organizations (e.g., TNCs) means shifting people to different cultures and raising some problem for host governments, local employees, and families of those who travel.

SCIENCE, TECHNOLOGY, AND PRODUCTION

New production technologies (e.g., based on the microprocessor)
may accelerate a move towards capital-intensive, large-scale,
highly productive (in terms of labor productivity) production units
in many sectors.

How serious may the consequences be for employment? How
could such production processes best be adapted to the demands for
flexibility and personal control on the part of those who work on
them? What are the chances of a long-term capital shortage eventually limiting the scope for a move in this direction?

Another possibility is that in general the large, vertically in-
tegrated industrial firm may not be the most appropriate instru-
ment to exploit the opportunities provided by microprocessor and
electronics technology.

Will the organizational rigidity and inability to shift direction
quickly, if evident in a number of large corporations, make them
an easy prey for the new forms of small, flexible organizations that
may be quicker on their feet? Or again, may the electronic revolution encourage more decentralized patterns of living and working
(already true even within large organizations)? How might this affect the marketing, production, and employment processes of the
large corporation and the complex organization? Do considerations
of this kind point toward the possible emergence of a multisectoral
structure for the industrialized economy, on the following lines:

- A capital-intensive, highly automated, and highly productive
  sector, including big manufacturing industries and big commercial services like airlines, international banking, and
  telecommunications;
- A large-scale, labor-intensive service sector, including services
  like education and health;
- An entrepreneurial, small-scale sector, consisting of enterprises
  covering a very wide range of industrial, commercial, and nonprofit activities;
- An informal sector in which (generally speaking) work would
  be unpaid, voluntary, and often difficult to distinguish from
  leisure.

How likely is the emergence of a "plus-industrial" economy structured on these lines? How would the sectors relate to one another? How much movement would there be across their boundaries?

Questions about the social control of science and technology will almost certainly become more insistent. Without a more widely diffused understanding and consensus about the possible uses and impacts of new scientific and technological developments, we may get increasingly incoherent societal behavior — in the sense that continually rising demands for more technology-oriented growth and productivity may be accompanied by continually rising resistance to the social impacts of new technology. Moreover, unless the comparatively short-term commercial perspectives of business corporations and the comparatively short-term political perspectives of elected governments can be supplemented by effective pressures on behalf of long-term public interests, the research and development needed to meet foreseeable needs and problems may not get done in time.

What changes in technological decision-making may be needed here? The case of energy and other scarce natural resources, discussed earlier, may well be a typical example of this problem. How might they affect business management? In what ways can management contribute constructively to them?

The transfer of technology from industrialized to less developed countries is likely to raise increasingly urgent questions, especially for transnational corporations. The need for "appropriate" technology is becoming more widely discussed, as is the more controversial idea that the transfer of conventional industrial technologies often serves to perpetuate an economic form of neocolonialism. True, the assumption that the technologies used by industrialized countries are inappropriate for less developed countries will probably continue to be rejected by many ruling Third World elites who take their norms and models from the industrialized world. However, opinion in the industrialized world may already be starting to shift towards the view that conserving, humane, small-scale technologies are no less appropriate at home than they are in the Third World.

How may these contradictory and shifting perceptions affect

the prevailing approach to technology transfer, to the role of transnational corporations, and to the development and use of new technologies in both industrialized and Third World countries? Increasingly, technology transfer tends to become part of the two-way flow of international trade; probably we shall be seeing more managerial negotiations for transfer of technology in return for raw materials, energy, and perhaps work.

THE VULNERABILITY OF COMPLEX SOCIETIES AND THE NEED FOR A HOLISTIC, INTERDISCIPLINARY APPROACH

The complex, interdependent systems of modern societies are vulnerable to many different kinds of threat.

Industrial action may disrupt power systems, transport systems, water systems, and other comparable systems on which a country's whole economy may now depend. Terrorists may destroy key points in these systems. Accidents (e.g., at nuclear power stations) could create havoc. The complex patterns of international interdependency (e.g., for food and commodities) may be disrupted by climatic and other natural disasters, by political upheavals, or by war. Though there has always been vulnerability in human society, we have developed types and magnitudes of vulnerability today of a wholly different order from the past.

From now on we are likely to see increasingly urgent efforts to alleviate the dangers of major breakdowns (the insurance industry will play a role here). These efforts may take the form of new technical arrangements — for example, the provision of backup capability and redundancy in power, computer, and other systems. They may involve decentralization strategies as a matter of principle, based on a growing tendency on the part of people and organizations at every level to try to make themselves rather more self-reliant and rather less helplessly dependent for their vital necessities on remote, complex, vulnerable systems over whose operations they feel they have little control.

To some extent, once again, these possibilities seem to contradict and cut across one another. They will all be part of the future that faces management over the next thirty years, and they confirm the need for a holistic, interdisciplinary approach.

Management Response

This section deals with the management response to the challenges summarized in the previous section and makes some points about management education. What must be emphasized is the need to learn by doing, patiently, with an open mind and a respectful attitude towards the opinions and feelings of others.

MANAGEMENT AS A LEARNING PROCESS

Forecasting, in the sense of trying to predict with certainty what will happen in the future in order to adapt to it ahead of time, may become increasingly difficult and unwise. But forecasting in the sense of trying to understand future possibilities in order to influence them and in order to develop the flexibility needed to meet them will become increasingly important.

Forecasting the future, influencing it, and developing the flexibility to meet it can be seen as a never-ending process of learning in action, both for individual managers and for the organizations to which they belong. What forms of personal and organizational development does this imply? What contributions to it could be made by management education? Successful managers (and organizations) may need increasingly:

- To adopt an experimental, adaptive approach;
- To develop sympathy with people of different cultures and values;
- To be interested in the insights they can get from the history of past changes in society and from their experience of living in countries other than their own;
- To understand why change is so often perceived as threatening;
- To be curious about how values shift and how institutional forces work;
- To want to accelerate their own processes of learning.

These attributes may seem to conflict with the single-mindedness needed to get things done. How is this conflict to be resolved?

Management has hitherto tended to focus around the processes of economic rationality. The processes of science and technology on the one hand, and of politics and psychology (or societal and personal development), on the other, have become increasingly important. But they are still regarded as subordinate to management's main purpose. No one doubts that management may have to acquire new dimensions of understanding and skill in these areas. The more radical question is whether managers may have to learn to rethink their roles altogether. May they have to learn to reinvent their tasks, responsibilities, and functions, to redefine their priorities and goals within these new technological and political perspectives? For example, if authority is replaced by bargaining and hierarchy by contractual relations as the dominant context of management, the manager's role will become that of a social entrepreneur who combines not only material resources and knowledge but also social forces to achieve a desired result. Learning political skills will then become no less — perhaps more — important than learning conventional management skills. More dramatically, the management style of exerting influence may have to change from power in its different forms to nonpower — from formal power, sanction power, and even expert power towards open consultation.

BUSINESS, GOVERNMENT, AND RELATED INSTITUTIONAL QUESTIONS

Management should prepare itself for a continuing debate about the roles and structure of business and government and the relationship between them and for the continuing development and redefinition of those roles, structures, and relationships.

This fact gives rise to the following issues:

- For how long will the concept of a "corrected market economy" (or "mixed economy"), in which the economic functions of business are performed within a framework designed by government to meet wider social needs, remain useful and valid?
- Will the business corporation be increasingly expected to undertake social functions? Alternatively, may the accelerating automation of high-productivity industry result in a reduction of its social functions and in a creation of new institutions that will take responsibility for people who would otherwise be unemployed?

- Should management education for business managers and government managers be kept separate? Should they be combined? Should certain aspects (which?) be combined and others kept separate?

- The governance (including legitimacy, accountability, representational structure, control procedures, and ownership) of business corporations will be the subject of continuing debate. Employee participation, financial disclosure, composition of boards of directors, and many other specific issues seeking specific solutions country by country will continue to appear on the agenda. Transnational corporations will be especially exposed. We seem to be entering a period of search from which both new corporate and new governmental structures may emerge. What contribution should management aim to make to this debate and search? What contribution can management education make?

STRUCTURAL CHANGES

Management relationships based on authority and power seem likely, at least to some extent, to be replaced by relationships based on contractual links and personal understandings.

Decentralization, devolution, and the disaggregation of large organizations in both the public and the private sector lie in the future, at least to some extent. Patterns of work may become considerably more flexible. How can management prepare to handle changes of this kind?

In general, management seems likely to become more entrepreneurial.

In particular, social experimentation, innovation, and action learning will be more important. So will a more entrepreneurial approach to the financing and to the control of expenditure and work. Financing and control may both become more participative than they are today. How can the requisite new management skills and experience best be acquired?

MANAGEMENT OF CONSERVATION AND CONTRACTION

The management of conservation, which has been mentioned already, will become increasingly important.

How, for example, can management in the energy industries learn to help its customers to use less, not more, gas, oil, and electricity? What new management procedures and motivations will this imply?

The management of contraction will be no less important. First, many organizations will have to contract in size in order to become more effective. Second, organizations, like organisms, have always declined and died. This phenomenon may be a particularly significant feature of the next thirty years in order to restore dynamism to the economy.

Helping organizations to decline and die in good order may well become a more important aspect of management. How can managers be equipped for this? We are currently learning to do this for parts and pieces of an organization or a business (e.g., the notion of strategic portfolios of products), but not yet for the organization as a whole.

HOLISTIC/PLURALISTIC APPROACH

Almost all that has been said has stressed the need for management to deal with the finance, personnel, marketing, production, technical, and social functions of management, not as specialties in separate compartments, but as interrelated aspects of the single management task. At the same time, we have stressed that many different types of people will be needed as managers and many different roles will be played by managers — for example, operations managers, support specialists, organizers and leaders, innovators and entrepreneurs, service managers, nonprofit managers, politicians-statesmen, trustees, communicators, and negotiators. There is a whole family of needs to be met and skills to be mastered. No one individual is likely to cover them all. No one form of management experience and education is likely to cater to them all.

How can management best meet these holistic/pluralistic needs? And how can management education best contribute? The international settings and cross-cultural pressures will force TNCs — whether they like it or not — to respond to pluralistic, nationalistic regulations and differentiations.

A NEW IDEOLOGY FOR MANAGEMENT?

Is the work ethic on the way out? What about the growth ethic and the profit ethic? We may know in thirty years' time. Certainly, it seems possible that there will be great changes in the typical commitments and work styles of managers, the rewards they seek, the personalities they develop, and the ideology to which they subscribe. They are likely to spend much more time on person-to-person interaction than they are assumed to do at present and to be much more comfortable with uncertainty and multivalue situations. They are likely to recognize that how persons and societies use time is an indicator of their lifestyles, values, and priorities. They may have learned to limit their own time commitment to their managerial work and to play an active part in their own social environment. Many managers will probably have learned how to give managerial power away, how to enable former employees (or former parts of the corporation) to work independently, and how to develop new patterns of organized activity and of work based on arrangements of contract and trust.

This all points to the possibility of a new ethic or ideology for management — one that embraces the economic, technological, social, and political dimensions of the task. May the idea of self-development and self-discovery provide a new guiding principle for managers in their own lives? Could managers also find that enabling other people (including groups and communities) to develop and discover themselves provides them with a new guiding principle for their work? We need to consider whether enough talented people will be attracted by management and be willing to take on the tough role demanded — or whether some of the best young talent will be attracted to a new, nonwork ethic.

Is this the kind of possibility that management and management education can usefully pursue today? And if so, how?

MANAGEMENT (AND RELATED) EDUCATION

The whole of this volume bears on the future of management education/development. Below follow a few additional points:

1.   There is a real need for management to be provided with clear, alternative scenarios for those aspects of the future with which it is most concerned. These scenarios should be in a form that makes it possible to translate them into concrete implications for management. Is this a task that management education and research should perform?

2.   There is a growing need for management education to help with mid-life career shifts. The need will continue to grow. What forms of retraining, reeducation, and reorientation are required? We should determine whether it should be a separate endeavor from the formal, preexperience education or a sequential phase in a continuing process.

3.   How much management education should continue to take place in special centers of management education or within the organizations themselves? Should universities, community colleges, and schools also become centers for action learning and agencies for local development? We need to think about the role of research — the kind or type of research (i.e., basic, applied), who will be doing it, and what its focus and support will be. Should teachers in many places become animators and even organizers of socioeconomic activity? What continuing contribution can specialist centers of management education best make if management itself becomes generally more adaptive and experimental in its own approaches to action learning and social innovation?

4.   What should be management's role as regards public education on issues such as availability of resources, operation of market systems, distribution of income, international tensions, the uses and impacts of science and technology, the rigidity of institutions and alienation from them, the scope for more decentralized initiative and self-reliance? What should managers and management educators do to improve the education of the public about the realities of the management task? Where should the boundary between management education and public education be drawn?

CHAPTER 2

An Outline of Social Contexts and Questions

DANIEL BELL

In any social forecasting there are, it seems to me, certain logical procedures:

1. The stipulation of what *questions* one is asking, and why. These questions arise from:

- The historical context;
- Those hypotheses in social theory that stipulate directions of change (e.g., business cycles, shifts of geopolitical power, new social demands, and new values).

2. The definition of the relevant *arenas* and relevant *actors* within which these changes can be expected to take place.

3. The possible "undertows" that may change the character

29

of the arena and the kind and number of actors in the social situation. For example, almost all social theorists in the 1930s were focusing on the political and ideological conflicts in the Western world, the tensions of fascism, democracy and communism, and the possibilities of war. Few, if any, predicted the explosive and rapid breakup of the imperial and colonial system that produced more than 100 new nations in twenty-five years.

Efforts to write "integral" scenarios or to sketch "global models" are, I would argue, largely futile. The important procedure is to look at different kinds of social change in response to the different kinds of theoretical or political questions for which one wants answers. As a means of "structuring" such an approach, one should try to define "axial principles" and "axial structures" that provide the skeletal structures or the lines of division in a setting. One must look for social frameworks and structural contexts based on these axial principles. And one should "test for" undertows by seeing what underlying forces may be latent and could be eruptive under certain conditions.

The following pages are illustrative of these approaches. Each approach is, to some extent, dependent on the other. Yet one can work out each one in great detail and see them as "overlays" to be put together at different time periods from T_1 to T_n.

These notes are in three parts:

1. A sketch of the relevant historical context;
2. Some theoretical issues that derive from these contexts;
3. Different kinds of "social frameworks" that can be used as analytical contexts.

I. *Historical Context:* 1945–1975.

   A. The breakup of imperialism and the rise of new states. (Before World War II, 80 percent of the land mass of the world and 75 percent of the world's peoples were under Western domination; 25 percent of the land area and 25 percent of the peoples were under British rule.)

   B. The Great Power (Soviet and U.S.) political and ideological rivalry.

   C. The world economic boom for twenty-five years, averaging 5 percent in world production.

    1. The return of the German and Japanese economies.

    2. The industrialization of Italy and France.

    3. The industrialization of Brazil, Mexico, and the Southeast Asian archipelago.

    4. The expansion of the world middle class from 200 million to 500 million persons (Keyfitz estimate).

D. The establishment of a welfare-state principle in the Western countries.

E. The centrality of state direction or state management of societies and economies and the use of the political arena by disadvantaged minorities for economic gain.

F. The fragmentation of societies — ethnically, linguistically, communally, and tribally.

    1. The centrifugal forces of localism and nationalism in Europe.

    2. The tribal conflicts in Africa.

    3. The communal rivalries in Asia.

G. The passing of the charismatic leaders: Roosevelt, Churchill, de Gaulle, Adenauer, and, in the new states, Nehru, Sukarno, and Nkrumah.

H. The challenge to "authority" as a principle in Western societies; the questions of legitimacy; the loss of political authority by leaders in almost all states.

I. The expansion of military dictatorships — the military as the major organized force and the military as modernizers.

J. New political-economic clusters and power centers.

    1. European community.

    2. Mediterranean basin.

    3. Southeast Asia.

    4. Middle East.

K. The question of historically declining economies (e.g., Great Britain).

L. The resurgence of Islam as a religious and political force.

M. The rising challenge of the Third World in ideological (color or political) and economic terms.

N. The breaking up of Communist hegemony.

O. The weakening of American hegemony and the end of American exceptionalism.

P. The instability of the world economic and monetary systems.

II. *Theoretical Questions.* *

A. The "decline" or "crisis" of capitalism as an economic system and as a "social system" (legitimacy).

B. The governability of democracies — because of "overload," heightened tensions and conflicts, external threats, and loss of authority.

C. The limits to growth — material, energy, social.

D. The demographic trajectories in world, regional, and age-cohort distributions.

E. The coherence of the Communist bloc.

F. The possible weaknesses of the Soviet Union — agriculture, productivity, demographic imbalances, control systems by the Party.

G. Shifts in the loci of geopolitical power — from Europe and the United States to where?

H. Types and kinds of major technological changes with potentials for changing major economic and political relationships within and between states.

I. Areas of confrontation between the great power blocs.

J. Degrees and kinds of cooperation among Western interdependent nations.

K. The intractability of inflation as a structural problem.

L. The increasing diversity of lifestyles in the Western world and its consequences (e.g., discretionary social behavior) for its own societies and other societies.

M. The "spiritual" exhaustion of the Western world.

III. *Social Frameworks.*

A. The geopolitical relationships — the major "spatial" axes and the crucial strategic variables. * *

---

*These questions are meant to be illustrative and are loosely put. They are not specified as to the theory from which they are derived.

* *The spatial relationships are defined as to areas of conflict and cooperation and their time frames or intensity — for example, one would expect the East-West conflict to diminish in the 1990s because of (1) internal U.S. problems (e.g., productivity, demographic imbalances, problems of control) and (2) retreat of the United States from various arenas. The strategic variables all have different scales — for example, the energy problem as a 10-year frame; the age-cohort demographic problem as a 15-year scale.

1. Spatial axes.
   a) East versus West — the Soviet Union versus the United States.
   b) West versus West — the economic competition between the United States and Japan and Western Europe.
   c) North versus South — The Group of 77 versus the OECD countries.
   d) East versus East — Soviet Union versus China.
2. The strategic variables.
   a) Demographic transitions.
   b) Energy independence and costs.
   c) Mineral and metal resources.
   d) Agricultural status — food import or export; growth rates.
   e) Industrial-sector distributions within countries and growth rates and vulnerabilities.
   f) Science and technology capability.
   g) Military capability.
B. Issues.*
   1. The demand for a New International Economic Order.
      a) The Lima Target of 25 percent of world manufacturing in the UNCTAD nations by the year 2000.
      b) Commodity cartels of primary products.
      c) Type of new international division of labor.
      d) Possibilities of protectionism in declining Western countries (e.g., Britain).
   2. The demographic upheavals.
      a) In Latin America (with the exception of Argentina) 42–48 percent of the population is under fifteen years of age; what is likely to happen when this youth cohort enters the labor market and the university systems?
   3. The capital efficiency problem.
      a) What is the degree of reversal of capital-saving to capital-using ratios in Western countries, largely as a result of need for new energy replacements?

---

*These points are obviously illustrative, not exhaustive; yet I would say they are central issues.

    b) The effect on economic growth; the consequences to the science-based industries; the effect on R&D.
4. The heavy competitive rivalry of Southeast Asia plus Japan to Western capitalism — a major shift of economic locus.
5. The "imbalances" of the European system.
    a) France, Italy, and Spain becoming *industrialized* or industrial societies primarily after World War II.
    b) Germany as a heavy technological leader or "super-industrial" society.
    c) The expansion of postindustrial elements in the Western European economies (e.g., service sectors).
    d) The question of British decline — can it be reversed?

C. The postindustrial framework.
  1. The change in sectors and occupations.
    a) From goods to services.
    b) The rise of human professional services.
    c) The expansion of a professional and technical class (e.g., in the United States today one of every four persons in the labor force is classed as professional, technical, or managerial).
  2. The centrality of theoretical knowledge as the source of economic innovation and as the basis for formulation of policy questions.
    a) The expansion of the science-based industries (e.g., electronics, optics, polymers, and the specific products, computers, lasers, holograms, plastics).
    b) The role and costs of research as a collective good.
    c) A knowledge theory of value.
    d) The technical component of policy issues.
    e) The management of complexity.

D. Issues.
  1. Structural unemployment because of:
    a) Declining industries.
    b) Automation.
    c) Higher educational requirements.
  2. The loss of productivity because of the expansion of services and the built-in inflation potential.
  3. The strength capacity of the science and technology component of the society.

4. The underwriting of research as a collective good.
5. The challenge to "organizational forms" (e.g., the modern economic corporation became vertically organized as an adaptive form to mass production; it may be dysfunctional for the newer, more rapidly advancing technological industries).

E. Modal changes in infrastructure.
   1. Every society is tied together by three kinds of infrastructure.
      a) Transportation — roads, rivers, canals, railroads, airlines.
      b) Energy — water power, electricity grids, gas and oil pipelines.
      c) Communications — postal services, telegraph, telephone, radio, television, computer networks, facsimile, and so on.
   2. In the oldest system, transportation, most cities were located on the basis of water routes on rivers or on their usefulness as seaports. There is now underway a new "communications revolution" that will radically shift the centrality of interstructures. This results from the merging of telecommunications with computers — what Anthony Oettinger calls "compunications." One can foresee:
      a) Teletext systems — television screens and terminals for news, information, and services that replace newspapers, some libraries, and telephone purchase systems.
      b) Facsimile networks — transmissions of documents and even of mail by electronic means.
      c) Data processing networks — for example, electronic fund transfer, centralized order, invoice, scheduling, and program procedures.
      d) Interactive networks for on-line research procedures.
      e) Larger command-and-control systems in the military organizations.
   3. Issues.
      a) The potentialities for the greater centralization of power.
      b) The rise of new types of "transaction, accounting, and processing" firms (e.g., the expansion of banks into data processing firms).

    c) Role of and control of large information data banks and retrieval systems.

F. The matching of scales.

  1. The new infrastructures and postindustrial frameworks create new arenas and scales (e.g., a world economy in which information, such as money rates, is available in "real time" in twenty-five different money markets).

  2. The crucial question (one that needs more space than is available here to sketch out all of the qualitative problems) is the matching of functional scales, within and between nations; as I formulated in an essay in *Foreign Policy:* "The National State has become too small for the big problems of life and too big for the small problems."

G. New technological changes.

  1. Automation — the possibilities for the first time of full-scale automation through numerically controlled machine tools and through microprocessors.

  2. Materials science — the fact that materials scientists no longer think in terms of specific metals or resources (such as copper, tin, aluminum, steel) but of the *properties* necessary for the structure or system (e.g., conductors, resistors, and insulators in electrical systems); expansion of this science means that "substitution" outmodes all resource problems.

H. Master keys.

  1. The great masters of the social sciences, Marx, Tocqueville, Weber, often had a large single vision of major changes as deriving from single axial principles. Thus, for Marx, the axial principle of capitalism was commodity production. For Tocqueville, the axial principle of democracy was "equality." For Weber, the axial principle of industrial society was "rationalization." Are there any master keys one can see that will "unlock" future developments? Some candidates are:

    a) The centrality of color.

    b) The desire for decentralization of societies — and the corollary, the attack on bureaucracy.

I. Modal historical shifts in "empires."
   1. What we have seen and do not wholly understand is that societies or nations at times display great "energies" and then decline; in the modern world we have had Spanish, French, and British empires. Are there new "empires" on the horizon? China? Is there a major geohistorical shift to the Orient? Or to the Middle East?
   2. Will we see the expansion and, in some cases, revival of "Pan" movements — Pan-Arab, Pan-African, Pan-Slav, Pan-Han?

These questions take us, however, far beyond the horizon of the twentieth century.

CHAPTER 3

The Challenge of Development: A Prospective View

IGNACY SACHS

Problems of the Present Age

Ours is, hopefully, an age of discontinuity. The worst possible course for the remainder of the century would be to continue the wasteful growth patterns of the postwar period. This applies equally to the North and to the South, as well as to the North-South relations.

THE NORTH

The average Northerner enjoys today, it is true, unprecedented material comfort. Conditions have enormously changed as compared with the thirties, and the devastating effects of war have been wiped off even in those European countries that suffered most. The average conceals, however, a broad spectrum of situations, including significant pockets of poverty, deprivation, and dependency. Our societies are inequality-ridden, as illustrated by racial discrimination, inequality between sexes, marginalization of the old and of the youth, not to speak of the income differentials.

More significantly, affluence did not buy general happiness. Many people feel alienated by conditions of work and daily life. The megamachine frightens them, and so does the megabureaucracy. They belong to the lonely crowd of TV watchers, our joyless society. A quarter-century of rapid growth made us tremendously rich but, at the same time, wasteful to the point of creating a cluster of structural problems or crises. One is the abusive rate of exploitation of nature. We are taxing it too heavily, depleting the stocks of nonrenewable resources, dumping our refuse and dissipating heat. For how long can we go increasing the scale of our activities without reaching a danger zone, if not "outer limits" altogether?

I do not have at all an apocalyptic view of the impending ecological disaster by means of depletion of resources and/or generalized pollution. Two less remote scenarios of doom are the failure of a megamachine (say, electric power system) in conjunction with a natural disaster and, of course, nuclear war by accident. Yet we must learn to live in a finite world and act in conformity with ecological prudence. We cannot lightly dismiss the risk of adversely affecting the climate by dissipating too much heat from fossil or fissile fuels. In practical terms this means increasing the efficiency of energy and resource use, eliminating, or at least drastically reducing, the socially most wasteful resource uses such as armaments, and giving a fairer access to potentially scarce resources to those people and nations who up to now have been deprived of them.

Another problem stems from the spatial maldistribution of people, industries, and wealth. Industrial congestion, heavy concentration of the population in metropolitan areas and big cities, and the progressive abandonment of the countryside make us lose at both ends: The quality of urban life deteriorates while former agricultural areas, cultivated for centuries, are allowed to become wasteland.

Of all the forms of wastefulness, the worst is the one that affects people. Unable to control the directions and the pace of technological progress, we suffer today from important structural unemployment, the most hard hit being young people in the sixteen-to-twenty-five-year-old age bracket, women, and minorities. Most technological forecasts anticipate further rapid increases in the productivity of labor, brought about by technical progress and labor-displacing rationalization investment stimulated by the growing struggle for external markets. The situation can only worsen unless measures are taken to reduce working hours and to distribute more equitably the total load of work.

As for the more or less elaborate welfare systems in existence in different countries, they certainly act as a useful cushion in the present employment crisis but hardly can be considered as a substitute for the effective guarantee of the right to earn a decent income by work. To live on welfare means to be reduced to a state of dependency that often has devastating moral effects. Moreover, our welfare systems are crumbling under the weight of their mounting cost and bureaucratic inefficiency. This should not be taken as an invitation to dismantle the welfare services. They should stay as they are while we look for meaningful alternatives and put these to test by means of life-size experimentation. Social services of different kinds (e.g., taking care of children or old and sick people) could perhaps gain in efficiency as a predominantly nonmarket, self-managed service at the family/neighborhood/community continuum level. The role of the state would consist in guaranteeing to the local group access to resources (including expertise) not available on the spot.

The development of the collective household sector (or shall we call it "domestic sector"?) offers a perspective in many ways opposed to the vision of a market-dominated, service-oriented postindustrial society.

THE SOUTH

Let us turn now to the *South*. As a whole it can boast in the postwar period impressive rates of growth and modernization — the latter understood as the setting up of powerful technobureaucracies, mod-

ern plants, huge cities, and armies equipped with costly and sophisticated weaponry.

The record is still more impressive in the realm of international
balance of power. The Third World is today a reality to contend
with, in spite of its many weaknesses, internal contradictions, and
bonds of dependency. The year 1973 was in this respect a watershed, as the Third World realized the power of physical control
over a strategic resource and, as a consequence, the possibility of
achieving over time a meaningful and mutually beneficial pattern
of interdependence with the North. The 1975 attempt to challenge
the present international order should be seen in the historical perspective as the first in a sequence of collective moves by the majority of UN members to question the global system in which we
happen to be as a result of three centuries or so of Northern domination over the world.

The setback in the negotiation of the New International Economic Order (NIEO) is certainly a tribute to the skills of our dip-
lomats and a monument also to our shortsightedness. These
dilatory tactics may yet cost us a major strategic defeat. In the early
fifties Stalin could not pursue his design of splitting the world
economy into two parallel markets because he did not have in hand
any economic leverage to pressure the West. The situation would
be quite different with a militant and abused Third World deciding
to delink from the North and going ahead on the basis of collective
autarchy. Though conceding that such a prospect is unlikely, I still
fail to understand why the North has taken such a negative stance
toward the NIEO, which, stripped of its verbal utterances, does not
purport to change in a fundamental way the present international
division of labor. Introducing a measure of stability on the commodity markets would be mutually beneficial, and it is time to
admit that the present distribution of gains from trade with the
Third World cannot be sustained. Gregory Bateson, the anthropologist, has warned us that the most likely paradigm of self-destruc-
tion for civilizations is lack of flexibility — becoming prisoner of
short-term interests that will backfire in the long run.

Having said this, we must look beyond the GNP growth figures.
Particularly striking with respect to the Third World is the terrible
and, on the whole, worsening maldistribution of income between
countries, regions within countries, and social groups. The gap has
tremendously widened between "capital surplus" oil-producing
countries (which should not be mistaken for the whole OPEC

group), the so-called newly industrializing countries, and the poor, resource poor, and/or landlocked countries of Africa and Asia. The picture is the same if one compares the capitals and the richest provinces with the poorest within one country — say, Sao Paulo with Piaui in Brazil. Finally, the benefits of growth and the blessings, some of them problematic, of modernization bypass a substantial part, if not the majority, of the population — the rural and urban poor — while the main beneficiaries belong, whatever the case, to the top 1, 5, or 10 percent income bracket. This upper class has been tremendously successful in imitating, emulating, and even surpassing the Northern lifestyles and wasteful consumption patterns. Thus, maldevelopment in the South comprises features shared in common with the North with other features that are unique to the South — the worst of the two worlds, so to say. On the one hand, the South must deal with the Northern problems of urban congestion, mass automobile traffic, pollution, and wasteful patterns of resource use, imported through the imitative growth model of the elites; on the other, with tremendous social inequalities, appalling misery, mass unemployment and underemployment both among the rural and urban populations. To these problems one should add environmental disruption arising out of poverty and uneven access to land, as well as out of predatory exploitation of forest and other resources; obsession with growth on the part of governments plagued with balance-of-payments deficits, careless and shortsighted policies of transnational corporations (TNCs), and anachronic agrarian structures.

NORTH-SOUTH RELATIONS

Thus, the present can be described, in spite of (or because of) savage growth in the past, as a conjunction of maldevelopment crises in the North and in the South. The picture is also bleak at the interface between the North and the South. The present division of labor and distribution of gains from trade is seen by the South as a stumbling bloc on its development path. The situation will not improve by paying lip service to free trade while raising protectionist barriers and encouraging some Third World countries to engage in an outward-looking, shallow industrialization aimed at exploring the competitive advantage of cheap labor. The only winners in this game may be the TNCs involved in South-North trade. But exports of cheap-labor manufactured goods cannot be a substitute for land reforms and a genuine development strategy based on a continuously expanding internal market and on collective self-reliance, which should not be mistaken for autarchy, among Third World countries. After 1973 the industrialized powers succeeded in compensating for the increased oil bill by additional exports to Third World countries of capital goods, turn-key factories, and know-how. But such exports are financed by recycling petrodollars deposited in our banks by capital-surplus oil-producing countries, while the indebtedness of the remaining Third World countries has been growing at an alarming rate. Moreover, a substantial part of the supplied equipments will soon start to produce for export, as the importing countries are unable, unwilling, or too small to cater to an expanding internal market. More turbulence is to be expected in this way for the world economy, already disturbed by the sharp struggle among leading industrial powers.

The present pattern of North-South relations thus depends on the continuing recycling of petrodollars and on the acceptance of the tyranny of the IMF on the part of the indebted Third World countries, who are constantly reminded of the need of sacrificing to short-term balance-of-payments considerations their long-term development interest. Neither of these conditions should be taken for granted: The capital-surplus oil-producing countries are being urged to explore the forward and backward linkages between their economies and those of newly industrializing countries. A revolt against IMF interference in internal matters of the Third World (and not only of the Third World) countries is only a matter of time. Above all, the North should realize that its own long-term enlightened interest requires a more balanced and socially equitable development of the South, primarily oriented toward expanding internal markets and collective self-reliance, and ready to engage in a selective and mutually beneficial interdependence with the North. This may entail costs for us in the short run and require giving up the idea of keeping the quasi-monopoly of the North in science-based and qualified-labor-intensive goods and technical services. As a matter of fact, countries like India already have a comparative advantage in such services because of the abundant supply of skilled manpower and of the low wage line.

Dimensions of Development

If my reading of the situation is correct, it would be folly to try to overcome the maldevelopment crises by more of the same — that is, by rapid growth, projecting into the future the trends of the past. At best, the outcome would be an *apartheid* postindustrial economy in the North, an *apartheid* industrializing economy in some countries of the South, and an *apartheid* international economy linking the North to the South. The charitable assumption is that an ever more productive minority would strive to keep under control the forcibly idle minority by means of a generalized and paternalistic welfare system. A less charitable assumption is that repressive regimes and wired fences would be required. Fortunately enough, a *fuite en avant* by means of an acceleration of the present growth patterns seems unlikely. As usual, the reference projection is a poor tool for forecasting.

I consider as even more unlikely and undesirable the no-growth alternative to growth with maldevelopment. So long as there remain rich and poor people and rich and poor nations, absence of growth can only increase the social inequalities. Besides, the rate of exploitation of nature does not depend on the rates of growth as much as on the contents and modality of growth and the distribution of its fruits.

The real challenge, both in the North and in the South, is to seize the opportunity of the present crises and to search for transition strategies from maldevelopment to genuine development, giving each one of us and all of us an opportunity of fulfilling ourselves by designing and pursuing individual and collective projects (in the Sartrian meaning of the word).

Ours is already an age of plenty, at least in the North. If we succeed in self-controlling our material needs, we should be able drastically to reduce the time spent in professional work and increase instead the time devoted to the direct nonmarket production of social services and other use values already referred to, as well as to all sorts of cultural, creative, and convivial activities. Our lifestyles would undergo, in this way, a deep change and would, one hopes, become considerably richer, more challenging, and more interesting. Development may be viewed in its initial stages as a liberation process — from want, fear, and dependency — and then as a societal learning process whereby people learn to identify their pluralistic and multidimensional value scales and diversified needs and engage in projects whose variety reflects not only the diversity of cultural and ecological contexts but also human inventiveness. Our freedom can be measured by our ability to shape our lives in a unique way and to invent a future different from the past. History should be scrutinized for antimodels to be overcome, never for models to be copied.

Development is also an ethical concept underscored by the twin and inseparable principles of synchronic and diachronic solidarity with our generation and the generations to come — that is, by the need for social justice and ecological prudence.

Finally, development has an aesthetic dimension. Beauty, joy, and quality of life are all facets of development, albeit they do not fit easily into the reductionist, narrowly quantitative discourse of economists and planners. It is the discourse that must change. We must learn to reason directly on use values without passing through the exchange (market) value. For this we should be ready to give up the comforting but illusory universe of optimality established by means of appropriate algorithms and, at the same time, outgrow the obsolete market mentality. Development choices are always politic; they are a citizen's affair. The transition from maldevelopment to development calls for the curbing of megabureaucracies, technostructures, and giant corporations and a redistribution of the balance of power between the state, the market, and civil society in favor of the last. Three qualifications are in order here:

1. The strengthening of civil society and the broadening of the space for local autonomy is not a call for counterculture and for the setting up of self-contained communities that turn their backs both on the market and the state and voluntarily choose to live at the margin of society. Counterculture is an important symptom of the present malaise, and in the pluralistic world of my dreams there should always be room for it. But it does not prefigure the shape of future policy. Our complex world cannot and should not be resolved in an archipelago of isolated communities. The case is altogether different when civil society takes the initiative, usually to cope with a crisis that was not assumed by the institution(s) supposed to deal with it. If the local group is entirely successful, it becomes a sort of counterpower capable of negotiating with the state, and the market forces a concrete solution to a specific problem. Therefrom it can move to another problem, releasing grassroot creativity, or else dissolve itself, considering that the goal that prompted the action has been achieved. The institutional dynamics

of civil society in constant motion differ sharply from the strait-
jacket of self-perpetuating state bureaucracy.

2. Insistence on grass-root citizen involvement as a condition
for self-reliant, endogenous, and need-oriented ecodevelopment
must go hand in hand with the redefinition of the functions of the
state and of overall development planning. While maximizing the
scope for grass-root autonomy through appropriate legal measures,
the state should grant access to critical resources that are not locally
available and favor networking among parallel experiments. At the
same time it should contextually influence local decisions by designing and implementing energy, space-use, resource, and technological policies. The aim of such policies would be to ensure their
conformity with an overall long-term interest based on expanded
social rationality and not on narrow market criteria. A possible
practical way of achieving these goals might be selectively to support by loans, grants, fiscal advantages, and technical assistance
local development-program contracts negotiated between all the
social actors. Contextual, contractual, and advocacy planning complement each other.

3. The vision of decentralized ecodevelopment striving to de-
bunk megabureaucracies, technostructures, and megamachines is
not directed against science and technology as such. It postulates
a firm social control on science and technology. Neither military
nor narrow economic criteria suffice to assess the multivarious
societal and ecological impacts of present or future technologies.
Whatever the complexity of issues involved, ordinary people should
be fully informed and invited to discuss them. Technology assessment belongs to the body politic, not to the technocrats. Ecodevelopment means taking full advantage of the unfolding possibilities
of science (e.g., to make the widest possible use of renewable resources on a sustainable basis). All the same, progress in telecommunications may help to turn into reality the up-to-now theoretical
paradigm of a decentralized yet articulated, complex, and sophisticated civilization — on the condition, however, that data processing will become a public service rather than the monopoly of
a few giant corporations and that effective access to data banks will
be democratically granted to everybody.

Transition Strategies

Where shall we stand at the turn of the century? Somewhere between the catastrophic reference projection of a world of *apartheid*

and the voluntaristic, normative, ideal, but not altogether impossible, construction just outlined. How far in between will depend on our ability to use the present crises to depart from past trends. *Transition strategies* can and must get down to earth and address themselves to five sets of interrelated problems:

1.   We should make the best of the existing productive capacities while at the same time changing our lifestyles and consumption patterns to conform them with the aesthetic ethos of ecodevelopment. This calls for progressive and partial reconversion of many industries. A horizontal, grass-root dialogue among consumer associations, shop trade unions, and other bodies of civil society might be helpful in suggesting concrete reconversion paths.

2.   North-South relations should be thoroughly reassessed with a view to achieving a mutually acceptable regulated and planned interdependence, including a pattern of trade, changing over time, in which our partners will progressively export all sorts of industrial goods and not only cheap-labor manufactures. The main burden of adaptation lies on the North because of the present blatant asymmetry in the North-South relationship, our far greater elbow room for maneuvering and, also, the mental blinkers that prevent us from understanding the historical processes at work in world policy and economy. Up to now, in total misunderstanding of our enlightened self-interest, we have been doing our best to prevent genuine development in the South.

3.   The tasks outlined above will prove unfeasible unless we are ready to envisage global adjustment policies involving a reassessment of patterns of time uses of the society, welfare systems, and income distribution. The short-term costs of the NIEO must be equitably distributed if we want to prevent a coalition against the NIEO of powerful entrenched interests and the weakest sections of our population.

4.   We must give urgent thought to ways of institutionalizing permanent and democratic citizen control over science and technology.

5.   Concerted international action is required to manage in an ecologically prudent way the so-called international commons — oceans and the seabed, the climate, and outer space. Little has been done to institutionalize these concerns, in spite of the Stockholm Conference and the efforts displayed by UNEP. The Law of the Sea Conference is playing havoc with the idea of using the seabed minerals and other wealth belonging to "the common heritage of mankind" as a source of independent and automatic funding of UN development-oriented activities. The setting up of a supranational

world authority is unlikely and would not be of much help so long as the North does not learn to live within a UN dominated by a Third World majority. Fresh thinking and institutional design are urgently needed in the whole area of global management of world resources.

Beyond these concrete tasks, we must change our ways of thinking, learn how to use our freedom of shaping the future, and learn how to become at least humans. This is by far the most difficult and challenging task ever faced by mankind — the biggest mental revolution yet to come.

CHAPTER 4

Sectoral Composition of GNP and Educational Composition of the Labor Force: The Coming Thirty Years

JAN TINBERGEN

Forecasting is a very risky activity, in particular because of the political uncertainties and the uncertainties in technological development. The generally known illustration of the latter is the impact that chips will have on the expansion of automation and the impact of expanded automation on the demand for new services as a consequence of their lower price after further automation.

Among the factors on which we have some better information is the so-called Fourastié effect. Jean Fourastié (1949) defended the thesis that the role of manufacturing industry would show the same evolution as had been shown before by agriculture — that is, it would require a decreasing portion of the national labor force and contribute a decreasing portion to GNP. Some figures drawn from Leontief's (1977) study about the future of the world economy constitute one way of illustrating this tendency (see table 4.1).The process of a decline in the percentage of GNP derived from manufacturing can be shown to have already started between 1960 and 1974, although not in all industrialized nations (see table 4.2). More details about individual manufacturing industries can be found in table 4.3, derived from Leontief's (1977) study.

It seems worth mentioning that in this scenario, the average rates of growth of GNP per capita over the period 1970–2000 have been assumed by Leontief to be 2.27 percent for North America, 3.22 percent for Western Europe (high), 4.23 percent for the Soviet Union, and 4.00 percent for Japan. In comparison to the growth rates prevailing between 1950 and 1970, these figures are modest; even so, many environmentalists will wonder whether the figures are not too high. Personally, I hold that opinion, and one of the reasons is that at present the average consumption per capita of meat, sugar, alcoholic beverages, tobacco products, and drugs is already higher than is optimal for our health. Such arguments for

Table 4.1   Per Capita Income and Percentage of GNP Derived from Manufacturing in the Main Industrial Regions in 1970 and Leontief's Forecast for 2000

	1970		2000	
Region	Per Capita Income (1970 dollars)	Manufacturing % of GNP	Per Capita Income (1970 dollars)	Manufacturing % of GNP
North America	4625	27	9067	20
Western Europe[a]	2585	32	6685	23
Soviet Union	1791	27	6212	23
Japan	1916	27	6223	23

Source: Leontief (1977).
[a]Countries with relatively high incomes, as defined in Leontief (1977). See also Tinbergen (1978).

Table 4.2   Percentage of GNP Derived from Manufacturing in 1960 and 1974, Selected Industrial Countries

Country	1960	1974
Belgium	30	31[a]
Canada	23	20
Denmark	29	27
France	40	36
Germany (Fed. Rep.)	42	40
Great Britain	32	26
Italy	34	34
Netherlands	34	29
Sweden	27	29
United States	28	25[a]

[a]1973 figures.

a slower growth of material consumption only reinforce the argument to be presented in what follows — the argument in favor of rapid growth in a number of services.

By general definition, the word *services* usually indicates a number of activities not classified as primary (e.g., agriculture and mining) or secondary (e.g., manufacturing industry, construction and public utilities). Both Fourastié (1949, 1978) and Bell (1973) emphasize the future role of the services sector in the so-called postindustrial society. The phrase *services* covers a very heterogeneous group of activities, and it is desirable to make a distinction between traditional and modern services. Among the former we have domestic services, important in poor countries but almost disappearing until recently as a gainful occupation in prosperous countries. The changing pattern of norms concerning jobs for males and females may make for some reappearance of paid domestic services (when wives claim a salary from their husbands) or of domestic work being done by both sexes. Among traditional services we also have trade and transportation and some sorts of banking, including money-lending in poor countries. Modern forms of services include, to begin with, modern techniques of traditional services. Among them are mechanical housekeeping (servants coming in cars, using vacuum cleaners, (dish) washing machines, etcetera), trade in supermarkets, transportation by container ships, aircrafts, or Japanese trains. The banking subsector uses modern equipment and has been extended by a growing insurance subsector

Table 4.3 Output Levels of Selected Manufacturing Industries in 1970 and 2000 for North America and Western Europe

Industry	North America		Western Europe	
	1970	2000	1970	2000
Food processing	71	142	48	127
Petroleum refining	19	45	9	13
Primary metals	40	125	26	99
Textiles, apparel	37	104	45	93
Wood and coal	14	35	10	23
Furniture, fixtures	9	23	28	19
Paper	24	74	13	55
Printing	27	75	13	59
Rubber	17	44	8	42
Industrial chemicals	26	72	20	70
Fertilizers	17	28	15	31
Other chemicals	24	61	15	67
Cement	2	8	1	7
Glass	21	65	13	57
Motor vehicles	44	108	26	122
Aircraft	14	41	4	13
Other transportation equipment	7	20	5	14
Metal products	63	172	33	136
Machinery	53	139	41	147
Electrical machinery	45	117	25	113
Instruments	10	28	6	25
Other manufactures	10	28	11	31

Source: Leontief (1977).
Note: Only those Western European countries with relatively high 1970 incomes are included.

— not only private but increasingly public social insurance. The frontier with the government subsector (which also existed under primitive circumstances, of course) has become blurred when it comes to social security agencies that are forms of insurance only in name. In addition, modern forms of services include many more government activities as well as mixed private activities in the fields of education, research, and newer forms of medical services.

It is in these modern types of services that we have to look for the growth activities. This does not mean that some subsectors of secondary activities will not also contain growth elements. Clearly, continuous further changes in qualities of products and the appearance of new products will go on. One example of the latter is the antipollution equipment that will be necessary and hence required, in part, by new legislation. I cannot agree with what has been expressed somewhat bitterly on this issue by Landau (1978).

What we have called modern services consist of four categories: (1) education, (2) research, (3) social services, and (4) other government services. The indication "other" is desirable, since sometimes important parts of the other categories are taken care of by public or mixed public-private agencies. Some comments on each of the four categories are given below:

1. *Education* has expanded considerably for two main reasons: It is both a consumption item desired as a consequence of higher prosperity and an investment activity. The latter is a consequence of an increased demand exerted by the "organization of production." This may be illustrated by the levels of education required in the main sectors of activity. Table 4.4 gives figures for the Netherlands, and they are representative of many industrialized countries. Table 4.5 gives figures for the United States for 1976 and also includes an official forecast for 1990. It shows that the expansion of education is expected to continue — a phenomenon also expected elsewhere (e.g., in the Netherlands).

2. *Research* is not only done in specialized research institutes but also in educational and other subsectors. Its significance is quickly rising. By the way, this rise illustrates that the assumption of complete information available to all economic actors, silently or openly made by economic science, is highly unrealistic. The role of information has been recognized step by step. One of the central questions on information in economic activity is whether it should be stored in a centralized or in a decentralized way. Up to a point, countries with an imperative central plan try to apply centralized storage. Free-enterprise market economies apply a fair degree of decentralization. Complete centralization is hardly conceivable, and so far the so-called centrally planned economies have experienced considerable disadvantages from it. Even so, the rapid development in information systems does cause shifts and implies at least some tendency toward more centralization. An even more important aspect of research is that in the last decades we have learned how much less we know than we thought we knew. The problems of human environment and other problems taken up by

Table 4.4 Percentages of Manpower with Various Levels of Education for Some Sectors and Subsectors in the Netherlands, 1975

Sectors or Subsectors		Level of Education					
	Elementary	Extended Elementary		Secondary		Third-level	
		General	Vocational	General	Vocational	Semi	Compl.
Agriculture	42	3	41	0	1	1	0
Manufacturing	42	9	32	3	8	4	1
Trade, tourism, repair	37	16	30	4	9	3	1
Transport, communication	42	16	26	4	9	3	1
Banking, insurance	15	28	14	11	18	8	6
Other services	20	12	17	4	18	19	9
Education	11	10		14		49	17
Research, other	15	27		21		18	19
Social services	28	29		30		11	6
Other government services	17	43		26		8	6

Source: Central Bureau of Statistics, partly by courtesy of Dr. H. de Groot (Social-Cultural Planning Bureau).

Table 4.5   Percentage of U.S. Labor Force with Various Levels of Education, 1976 and Forecast for 1990

| | Level of Education | | | | | | | |
| | Elementary | | | High School | | College | | |
Year	Less than 5y	5–7y	8y	1–3y	4y	1–3y	4y or more	Total
1976	3.9	7.1	9.7	15.3	36.3	13.0	14.7	100
1990	1.8	3.7	5.9	14.7	39.9	14.8	19.3	100

Source: *Statistical Abstract of the United States* (1977, p. 137). For 1990, figures are an average of a low and a high estimate.

the Club of Rome have contributed a lot to our drastically changed views on these matters and stressed the enormous need for more research. Alongside environmental questions are those of food scarcity in some parts of the world and the burning question of how to save on energy and to find new, not too risky, forms of energy.

3.   *Social services* as we define them include medical services as well as a large group of other forms of assistance to people in difficulties, material or spiritual. With increasing well-being, societies are able and willing to organize such assistance instead of leaving it to paternal and other forms of charity. There are differences of opinion on the limits, however. Charity, to the extent it is known, was of the order of magnitude of 1 percent of national income in the nineteenth century. Social insurance and other forms of social security benefits in northwestern European countries are now at the level of some 30 percent, as compared with some 5 percent in 1938. In recent years important rises occurred as a consequence of unemployment. Conditions concerning the acceptance of other types of work or of retraining connected with the receipt of unemployment benefits are not sufficiently strong to maintain the work ethic a society needs in order to maintain the standard of living desired by the average citizen. The question may be put, however, whether in some respects the Western standard of life is not already too high. The crucial second question connected with the work ethic is, then, whether or not a higher degree of solidarity with Third World countries is necessary and is also in our own longer-term interest. These are good reasons to argue in favor of a considerably higher level of such solidarity.

4.   *Other government services* have also increased in variety and volume during most of the twentieth century. This implies

that the one-sided slogan of laissez faire has been replaced by attempts to analyze in a less detached way in what circumstances
private initiative can best be furthered by private ownership of the
means of production or in a decentralized way and in what circumstances other ways and means can be expected to work better. After
variegated and intensive discussions a number of tasks have been
identified that in most Western countries have been entrusted to
public authorities or to joint ventures of public and private bodies:

- Long ago Europeans did away with private armies and competing
  private central (i.e., note-issuing) banks. We also learned that
  the sheriff is to be preferred over the person acting as his or her
  own justice; not for so long, though, have these things been
  absent in the United States. Unfortunately, in recent years private violence for political objectives has been on the increase
  again, and perhaps more in Europe than in the United States.
  Certainly, the great majority of European citizens are against
  this tendency.

- In the Netherlands in 1902, the Dutch State Mines were established since not enough private capital was supplied. The same
  would happen around 1923 in Turkey's modernization process,
  guided by Atatürk — not the creation of mines but creation of
  the so-called state economic enterprises.

- In Europe, public utilities and rail transport were nationalized
  step by step, the main argument being that the alternative would
  be private monopolies, since free competition would lead to
  cutthroat competition (as indeed it did in American railways),
  not a very successful investment device.

- Ever since the Great Depression it has been understood that the
  avoidance of business cycles could not be seen as a private task.
  Similarly, we understand that unstable markets cannot be left
  to themselves either, and so most developed countries have
  agricultural protection or at least a policy of income guarantees
  to small farmers. (In fact, the system of subsistence payments
  previously applied in Britain is better than the EEC policy but
  more difficult to administer in some continental European
  countries.)

It is important to note a certain *parallelism* between the *supply of* and the *demand for* more highly qualified labor in the course of socioeconomic development. On the one hand, the educational system delivers an increasingly educated flow of alumni, and on the other hand, the organizers of production exert an increasingly high demand for more educated people. I want to express the hope that this increasingly schooled labor force will also turn out to be increasingly cultivated. So far developments are not so satisfactory. For a multiplicity of reasons — too numerous and also, partly, still too little known — the cultural level of our population in the deeper human sense is falling. Ortlieb (1971, 1978) and Mewes (1978) speak of irresponsibility, total egotism, and vanishing willingness to perform. I am afraid that, by and large, they are right.

There is concern among a number of observers and politicians about something else. They now must admit that there is some parallelism between supply of, and demand for, more qualified people, but they fear that there is not complete parallelism. They fear that an overproduction of highly educated people will show up and result in massive unemployment. For the Netherlands the demand for third-level manpower around 1990 has been estimated to be 6 percent of the total labor force lower than its supply. On the other side of the market, demand for first-level manpower has been estimated to be 6 percent higher than supply. For the middle level, demand and supply have been estimated to remain roughly in equilibrium.

These forecasts may be quite misleading. They do not seem to take into account the possibility of substitution of one type of labor for another as a consequence of relative salary or wage levels. In the last few years an increasing number of investigations on this subject have been made, and although our knowledge is very incomplete, my impression is that the elasticity of substitution between third-level and other (mainly second-level, of course) labor is of the order of magnitude of -1. (See Tinbergen 1975.) This implies that important increases in demand can be induced by sufficiently large relative declines in the salaries of the highly qualified. Apart from eliminating unemployment in the long run, this would also imply a wholesome contribution to the social climate. Wages of unskilled workers should rise in comparison to other wages and salaries, and high salaries should fall in comparison to other salaries. Such reduction of income differentials would also reduce the necessity to employ migrant workers. Of course, as a further complement, it requires a more forceful development policy in the countries from which the migrant workers are now recruited.

References

Bell, D. (1973). *The Coming of the Post-Industrial Society.* New York: Basic Books.
Fourastié, J. (1949). *Le grand espoir du XXe siècle.* Paris: Presses Universitaires de France.
———. (1978). *40 Ans de recherche.* Paris: Dalloz, Économie.
Landau, R. (1978). *Innovators and Entrepreneurs — An Endangered Species?* Washington, D.C.: National Academy of Engineering.
Leontief, W., et al. (1977). *The Future of the World Economy.* New York: United Nations.
Mewes, C., and H.-D. Ortlieb (1978). *Macht Gleichheid glücklich?* Freiburg in Breisgau: Herderbücherei No. 682.
Ortlieb, H.-D. (1971). *Die verantwortungslose Gesellschaft.* Munich: Godman.
———. (1978). *Vom totalitären Staat zum totalen Egoismus.* Zürich: Interfrom.
Tinbergen, J. (1975). "Substitution of Academically Trained by Other Manpower." Weltwirtschaftliches Archiv 111, Heft 3, S. 466–476.
———. (1978). "Les vingt-cinq pour cent pour le Tiers Monde." In Fourastié (1978), pp. 5–14.

CHAPTER 5

Environmental Trends and Internal Changes: Some Examples

DAVID CHAMBERS and MAURICE A. SAIAS

In the recent past, for less than twenty-five years, managers and management scholars have been concerned with the permanent adjustment of an organization's capabilities to its environmental requirements. Some progress was achieved when it was realized that these adjustments had to be somewhat anticipated. Long-range planning was born. Then the will to control the future of the organization and to make explicit choices was introduced, giving birth to strategic planning centered mainly on socioeconomic, technological variables and the choice of products/markets. It was a question of, "What business do we want to be in?" The rhythm of environmental change was within the reach of organizational response capabilities.

In the late sixties and the early seventies change accelerated and became more erratic. More variables were perceived as having an impact on business decisions. Sociocultural and political variables, external as well as internal, had to be considered. Acknowledgment of these factors led to the development of strategic management. Strategic management was the consequence of a period of novel discontinuities, unfamiliar to both managers and management scholars. In our era of weak signals and surprises, decision-makers are again turning to the futurologists for help.

Obviously, managers do not expect to get the "right answers" or a precise description of the future. Nonetheless, they would like to have an idea, however approximate, of possible evolution of the system they manage, in terms of external as well as internal demands. Managers will be able to make expert projections of possible future states of the world, drawing on evidence concerning economic and demographic trends, extensions in scientific knowledge, developments in technology, and so on. There is good reason for us to examine the evidence of current changes in the decision-making processes of business enterprises and to try to distinguish transitory changes from those that are going to persist. Indeed, we ought to be able to gain further insight into *which* of the possible states have some chance of materializing, if we examine current characteristics and current changes occurring in business enterprises. It is through these enterprises that the range of technical possibilities will be extended, and these are the agencies through which the changing aspirations of society will be met or will fail to be met. Hence there is a case for looking at the enterprises themselves, as well as at their changing environments. If you wish to estimate where a traveler will get to, it is helpful to know not only the nature of the terrain but also the characteristics of the vehicle he will be using.

Therefore, we shall first try to limit the terrain (i.e., the environment) and then look at some of the characteristics of the vehicle (i.e., the business enterprise).

Environmental Trends

Environmental changes are only of interest to business decision-makers to the extent that they impinge upon the businesses they manage or the way they manage them. Indeed, managers show little concern for variables that are not patently relevant. Unfortunately, relevance is difficult to recognize when the environment, as described by management practitioners and scientists, is turbulent, complex, heterogeneous, and made up of conflicting demands.

Futurologists are being given the responsibility of projecting not only the possible future state of the world but also the kind of implication future trends may have on business enterprises. Consequently, they are expected to broaden their own scope of investigation beyond the boundaries of their own discipline and analyze the interrelationships among the variables.

Management practitioners and scholars are aware of the fact that business is still a transformation process that must provide goods and services efficiently. But they are also aware that this role is no longer the sole criterion of their legitimacy. They are, therefore, convinced that attention should be devoted to any event that may have impact on the future of their markets, the resources they need, the transformation process, and the new legitimacy they have to gain. Among the variables they perceive as relevant and important, one can mention the following:

- General demographic and economic trends;
- Globalization of markets and economies;
- Shifts from products to services to information;
- Relations between industrial and industrializing societies:
  Transfer of "appropriate" technologies,
  Terms of trade,
  Development of national human resources;
- East-West relations;
- Shifting role of public and private management;
- Compatibility of egalitarianism with the market system;
- Quality of life:
  Materialism versus other values,
  Trade-offs within the limits of scarce resources;
- How individuals adjust to the changing value system around them, to work, to authority, to responsibility;
- Impact of trade unions on industrial relations.

It is almost impossible to isolate the consequences of each of these variables on management: The variables are so interrelated that their effects are themselves very closely intertwined. Their various impacts on management can be convergent or conflicting, and managers feel they will have to face constant paradoxes. Everyone will want more, and managers will feel that they are expected to satisfy everyone. Let us look at some of the questions they raise most frequently and at the consequences that some of these environmental trends may have on management.

POPULATION TRENDS

A few questions appear particularly crucial:

- In most Western countries birth rates are decreasing. Will they continue to do so?
- In these countries a larger proportion of the population lives to a greater age. Can we really expect the coexistence of four generations?
- What will happen to the current population growth in less developed countries?

GENERAL ECONOMIC TRENDS

- Will we have to live permanently with stagflation (i.e., high inflation and high unemployment rates)?
- Will we have to live with growth limitation due to energy, raw materials (including food), and capital shortages? Where are these shortages located — geographically, sectorally, and so on?
- What will happen in terms of national and international distribution of wealth?

WORLD MARKETS AND ECONOMIES

Managers tend to think that markets and economies are taking on a world dimension. How will this trend develop? In particular, how will it affect the East-West and North-South relations? International exchanges seem to increase along with a trend toward national specialization. Can these trends last, and what kind of specialization is to be expected? Terms of trade are deteriorating for the less developed countries. These countries are increasingly perceiving that technology is the critical element in the development process; they become more aggressive in their efforts to obtain it, mainly through multinational corporations. At the same time these countries are pushing for more local ownership and often for controlling ownership; at the very least they require that more nationals are utilized in senior positions.

Moreover, most governments in the less developed countries did not gain or maintain power through the democratic process. They feel the need to broaden their popular base, and one way to achieve popular support is through xenophobia. Managers are therefore wondering if their firms will be tolerated even when they can demonstrate economic value and "good citizenship." The growing unemployment rate in the developing countries may very well accentuate these previous tendencies. Managers do think that the globalization of markets and economies has domestic consequences.

DOMESTIC TRENDS

At home (i.e., in more developed countries) the situation looks very uncertain. If specialization becomes a leitmotiv, high technology, sophisticated services, and information will be the areas where the developed part of the world can keep its competitiveness. This means, however, a drastic shift in the present economic structure of several countries, especially in Europe. As a matter of fact, it will be harder to dissociate products from services or even production processes. Can we foresee the development of microprocessors, information and control systems, communications, biochemistry, and the like? How can we respond to these new opportunities when society resists these changes and calls on government to maintain the status quo beyond the point of no return?

We are going through a period of great change, similar to the industrial revolution. But as far as Europe is concerned, the race for the production of basic technology seems already lost or on the verge of being lost. Japan and the United States are the leaders.

Does Europe need to control the source of "components" that represent a minor proportion of the end-user devices or systems? Could we not concentrate on their conversion into marketable products, considering them as raw materials and bearing in mind that most products and production processes will have to change because of them?

What kind of social phenomena will be triggered by the new technologies? Experts maintain that the amount of work currently done by 25 to 30 percent of the active population could be achieved by only 5 percent in the near future. They also forecast drastic changes in our way of living, thanks to these technologies. The use of domestic computers is one of their favorite examples.

How are the governments going to react? Should we count on closer government/private sector cooperation? Does cooperation mean tighter government control and public interference? Or does it mean Japanese-style cooperation? How far will governments go in helping their national units to sustain international competition? Will they succumb to the temptation of protectionism? Or will they promote a drastic evolution of the industrial national structures?

TRENDS IN VALUES

Any evolution encouraged by the government or the private sector will have to take into account basic shifts in value systems. At present, demands are tending towards a more egalitarian society with an emphasis on quality of life and the restoration of the individual as such.

Economic well-being is, for a large part, taken for granted. Cultural, ecological, and social well-being make up the core of current demands. Will they be sustained if economic conditions worsen? What parts of these demands will be endorsed by politicians? Politics seems to absorb a larger part of our lives in certain countries, whereas people seem less and less interested in other areas. What can we expect in that respect? Should we be ready to invest in political forecasting? What degrees of freedom do the political parties have once they are elected and start to govern? Are not political processes more at play today in organizations at the microlevel than at the national level?

We have raised more questions than we have provided answers. We know what the present trends are, but we do not know whether or not they will continue. Assuming that they will, managers must get ready for the changes these trends will entail.

SOCIAL EMPHASIS

To perform economically does not guarantee legitimacy. Legitimacy will have to be gained through social and political credibility.

Social acceptance is internal and external. Externally, managers will have to accept some sense of public accountability by social reporting, a code of conduct, and social audit. They must be ready to respond to the proper concerns of society and at the same time speak up to explain what is being done, how, and why. They may even have to get involved politically to defend their legitimacy.

Internally, quality of management will be crucial and will start at the recruitment stage. Managers operating in the future will have to be motivated to ensure proper communications and to accept true participation — that is, to be ready to discuss problems and alternative solutions. They will have to be social leaders. In order to be able to achieve these conditions, organizations will have to be broken down into smaller units, humanly and socially manageable.

One can represent these constraints on management as shown in figure 5.1. The challenge faced by managers is that they will have

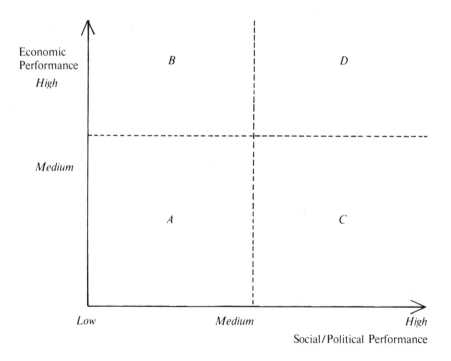

Figure 5.1. Challenges Faced by Future Managers

to achieve economic and technological as well as social and political performance.

In zone A, survival is jeopardized because the competitive standards required in the business are not met. To be below average under heavy competitive pressures is not sustainable in the long run.

In zone B, the managers are mainly economic achievers. Their organizational position is not stable. It will last as long as social and political pressures do not bring their economic performance below average. The solution for businesses located in zone B is to use part of their economic advantage to make social and political investment.

Economic performance of businesses located in zone C will prevent them from permanently meeting their social and political aspirations. Under economic pressure for survival, social and political performance will be reduced, thereby decreasing the organization's legitimacy. Sooner or later, businesses located in that area have a good chance to move toward zone A.

Businesses in zone D are the only ones guaranteed survival, provided flexibility is sufficient and they constantly adapt to new environmental demands. In principle, they can achieve this flexibility thanks to their competitive edge in economic, technological, social, and political terms.

To reach or to keep one's position in zone D is not automatic. It takes conscious competitive strategies that include social and political as well as economic and technological dimensions. Businesses in zone A are a sure source of trouble. Zones B and C are, at best, short transitory passages. Strategic tools such as the directional policy matrix will help in designing an optimal business portfolio — that is, in concentrating businesses in zone D. Managers using such techniques should be aware, however, that profitability can no longer be the main indicator of strategic success. Nevertheless, profit is still a primary measure of operational performance and a necessary input to strategic performance. Strategic performance should be evaluated by indicators of potential survival and viability in terms of creating, for a corporation, greater opportunities than are available to its competitors. These measures should evaluate the potential for increasing the corporation's future opportunities to commit its then available resources, and/or its potential for decreasing its opponents' future opportunities to commit their then available resources.

In evaluating potential, one should consider capacity to withstand heavy competitive pressures on domestic and international markets. As mentioned earlier, increased competition will come from industrialized and industrializing countries. The necessary specialization triggered by the globalization of markets should lead to a careful monitoring of the technological evolutions. Part of the potential of a corporation will be the quality of the technological watch it uses. The new industrial revolution is just starting. It will affect present products and production processes and create new products and production processes. Almost overnight it can lead to obsolescence and dramatic social and economic cost disadvantages. Moreover, we do not know the social or political consequences of this new industrial revolution. Again, decision-makers will have to emphasize flexibility and mobility. They must be ready for a new style of industrial relations and proactive societal and political attitudes.

Proactive attitudes are advocated in order to avoid politically motivated solutions that governments will impose to the detriment of all concerned — the employees, the employers, and society itself. The view that governments can solve problems — inflation or unemployment, for example — has been long-lived, at least as long-lived as the view of business as an optimizer. National policies, whether they are voluntary or statutory, cannot increase output or productivity or create jobs. Collective bargaining is an instrument for translating economic policies into improved performance and earnings. Employers and trade unionists will have to work closely with governments, taking proper account of the economy and of national interests in their collective bargaining.

When mentioning collective bargaining, we mean full and free collective bargaining. Workers' representatives need to have the full independence, the security, the information, and the training necessary to negotiate on behalf of their members. This implies disclosure of information, adequate time and facilities for education, and so on. But we also mean new and more imaginative forms of collective bargaining. Consumer organizations should not be ignored in agreements between management and unions or left out of conflicts in labor relations. Workers will seek the right to voice their opinions on issues like company policies and strategies. Denial of these rights may lead to endless conflicts.

A solution often advocated for successful and efficient bargaining is to restrict the size of organizational units in order to promote true participation, where problems and alternative solutions are discussed between managers and workers. Conflicts can be anticipated and avoided rather than solved or reduced, as is the case today. Small units can have clear objectives and a high degree of autonomy to decide how to achieve those objectives, and all members of the team can be involved in matters affecting them. In this type of participative management, workers will be treated as individuals — which is precisely what they will demand. Indeed, workers will tend to reject organizational structures in which they feel like cogs in an impersonal machine. They will accept organizational constraints only to the extent that they feel their personality, culture, social connections, et cetera, are taken into consideration.

The implication of these expected changes is that managers must be prepared to assume new roles. They will have to be social leaders of a cooperative type, able to work closely with their employees. Managers will have to spend a much greater proportion of their management time in communicating with employees. In order to do so, they will have to get rid of the clerical chores behind which many of them tend to hide. They will have to be harmonizers of coalitions — that is, in a certain way, political "animals." Trade unions and the labor force are already challenging managers to take up that role.

These political and social trends may be better understood and realized by looking at what is currently happening inside some European firms. The following section examines some internal changes currently taking place.

Some Current Internal Changes

The evidence we present here concerning contemporary changes in the management of certain business enterprises results from an experiment started recently by the British Social Science Research Council. In 1978 the SSRC launched a new scheme for research sponsorship, which it called "Open Door Research." This was intended to attract applications for research support from people outside the universities and polytechnics and to help practitioners to act as the instigators of research into problems of management and organization with which they had direct experience in the workplace. The proposals that quickly appeared in this channel offer a very interesting sample of current changes within business enterprises experienced by the participants and considered by them to have a wider significance. Three of these situations are described below.

LUCAS AEROSPACE COMBINE

The research proposal was aimed at identifying and analyzing the difficulties faced by a shop steward combine committee as it attempts to involve itself in the processes of corporate decision-making. The proposal for research was put forward by the Lucas Aerospace Combine Shop Stewards Committee, a body that links with the work force at seventeen sites in the United Kingdom and has been in existence since 1971. Lucas has been faced with the prospect of extensive redundancies in parts of its aerospace business, and one of the main initiatives of the combine has been to look for product diversification that will use existing skills and maintain employment. The combine circulated questionnaires asking for details of skills, plant, existing products, and possible alternatives; it commissioned reviews of the state of the art in fields of energy, transport, oceanics, and medical technology; it made attempts to relate the work force's skills to needs identified in various community groups. Altogether some 150 possible projects were suggested in the course of a year, and proposals were made for research and development to support some of these projects. The combine was instructed in fundamental issues of manpower planning, capital investment policy, and product development.

This search for diversification is now being monitored in the research that the combine has had funded through the Open Door scheme; the researchers are analyzing the difficulties and obstacles the combine encounters as it tries to take a role in the corporate decision-making process. These difficulties include an absence of marketing and financial expertise in the combine (i.e., starting from existing skills and plant, their approach is firmly rooted in production); its failure to win a place for its proposed alternative products and alternative production systems within existing collective bargaining negotiations; and its lack of official recognition from those trade unions with formal negotiating rights at Lucus.

One further aspect of the combine's experience calls for comment. In its early days the combine was aware of its general need for more and better *information*. As its interests subsequently developed to focus on product strategy and corporate decision-making, the emphasis tended to shift to the need for greater *expertise*. This shift must in turn pose important challenges to the systems providing services of education and research.

CHRYSLER U.K.

The research proposal was initiated by two bodies working together: the joint shop stewards negotiating committees from a number of Chrysler plants and the "Coventry Workshop," an independent educational charity working directly with trade union and community groups at local levels.

Chrysler U.K. is the only company in the United Kingdom to have entered into a planning agreement as defined in the Industry Act of 1975 — that is, a voluntary agreement entered into by a company and a minister of the Crown concerning the company's strategic plans for future development of any of its undertakings in the United Kingdom.

While trade unions are not parties to planning agreements, it has been clear that ministers would not approve an agreement unless prior consultation had taken place between the company and its recognized unions. Chrysler entered such a "voluntary agreement" as a condition of government aid in the course of the rescue operation of 1975. A Planning Agreement Working Party (PAWP) was formed, representing manual and staff unions and the company. This organizes its business through subcommittees on sales and products, sourcing and manufacturing, employment and productivity, and finance. It has immediately presented the Chrysler shop stewards with issues going well beyond the level of the individual plant, opening up major questions of corporate decision-making and offering the opportunity to initiate their own strategy alternatives for the firm and the industry. It also raises new requirements for the coordination of shop stewards' goals and tactics across diverse plants, among which the immediate interests of workers may often diverge. Again, trade union representatives on the PAWP find that their role in the PAWP may cut across their role in the collective bargaining process.

The negotiation of the Chrysler planning agreement is particularly interesting for the following reasons:

- The unions have attempted to win a place in the planning and decision-making process through the route of influencing government in a situation where company survival depended on government aid.
- The unions are aware that they currently lack knowledge and expertise to play the role as effectively as they would wish and are actively building the relevant competence.
- The initiative to take an active part in decision-making comes, in the case of Chrysler, from the unions rather than from a shop stewards committee (as in the case of Lucas).

POWER ENGINEERING INDUSTRY

The request for research support was put forward by the Power Engineering Industry Committee (PEIC). This is a body bringing together representatives from the joint shop stewards committees of the five major U.K. firms manufacturing turbine generators and boilers. While they come from different and competing firms, the committee members have a joint interest in defining a position on proposed structural changes in the industry and in influencing the ordering pattern of their major customer, the Central Electricity Generating Board (CEBG).

The U.K. electricity-generating industry has carried surplus capacity since the energy crisis of 1973, and the power manufacturers have had to face the prospect of significant contraction. The shop stewards PEIC has focused on two issues concerning the management of this contraction:

- Resistance to a proposal from the government's central policy review staff that existing manufacturers should merge: PEIC argues, for example, that the technologies of the two leading firms making turbine generators are different; that, as a result of a merger, one technology would be scrapped; and that there would be both a loss of jobs and a loss of essential experience and skills in the work force.
- Commitment by the CEBG to smoothing its forward ordering program.

The PEIC argument rests on two important premises — that maintaining the number of jobs is a primary objective and that maintaining the pool of skills accumulated in the work force is important in its own right.

Several interesting developments may be seen in this example. Groups of worker representatives are forming an alliance across separate (and competing) firms in order to address questions of strategy for their industry. One of their objectives is to alter the industry's environment, and one of the means they have chosen is to influence government, in turn, to direct the CEGB to choose a different course of action than would be selected if it were to consider only the specific objectives the CEGB has been charged to pursue. Again, the proposal for research support came from PEIC in collaboration with a specific group of researchers, the Trade Union Studies Information Unit. This is a research and information service to trade unions in northeastern England, wholly owned and controlled by affiliated T.U. branches and other T.U. organizations.

Conclusion

The three examples we have just reviewed may help us in discussion of several of our themes:

- *Rising expectations.* The change taking place is the unions' desire for a measure of self-determination, an active role in choosing the direction of the enterprise. In fact, this change goes beyond the union, in the first and third cases the active agent is not the union but the shop stewards.
- *Management responsibility and legitimacy.* What new kinds of joint corporate planning are emerging?
- *Egalitarianism and the market system.* It is significant that in each of the three cases the demand for a greater say in decisions about the enterprise's future has come in response to economic decline and loss of sales. The potential conflicts between shareholders' interests and those of other stakeholders (over such issues as job security and the maintenance of skills) have become explicit and actual in conditions of decline.

Our examples serve also to highlight questions whose relevance goes beyond these particular cases:

1. In Chrysler and PEIC the work force appears to have had access to routes for changing the firm's or industry's environment that were not readily accessible to management. Does this indicate new kinds of alliances in the pursuit of common interests and responses different from those usually predicted within a market system?

2. The cases display interesting differences. In the case of Chrysler the *opportunity* to play a central role in the planning process is there (and may well survive the Peugeot-Citroen takeover), but there is still a question about the unions' knowledge and expertise in a planning context. The Lucas shop stewards committee has impressive knowledge and expertise in many areas but has not won for itself the opportunity to use these within the company's own planning structure. To what extent will unions and shop stewards committees in the coming years build up their own expertise in company planning? To what extent will they create the opportunities to use such expertise?

3. The case of the PEIC illustrates collaboration within the work force across separate firms. Will this be an important feature of industrial activity in the coming years? What would be the implications for the economic and strategic choices of firms in these industries?

4. It is significant that both Chrysler and PEIC have developed stable relations with particular research groups outside the existing academic system: the Coventry Workshop and the TUSIU. These units, in turn, are now coming to demand, from the bodies through which the state sponsors and patronizes research, a share in the funds that have previously gone to university departments and official research establishments. Will there be a growing tendency to develop such activities outside the academic system and to blur the boundaries of the academic system by taking research work and the building of expertise out into the groups most affected by them?

5. What are the fundamental and durable interests of a work force that claims a greater role in corporate decision-making? The Lucas shop stewards' interest in socially useful technology is an attractive banner to march under, but is it more than that? The objective of job preservation is common to all three cases, but job preservation is not an absolute. Will the conditions under which a developed industrial society permits jobs to be eliminated become increasingly stringent? Will investment in skills be protected by constraining the adoption of new technologies? Will inventiveness in devising adequate means for compensating those whose skills are rendered obsolete keep pace with inventiveness in devising new technologies?

In this chapter we have attempted to point at some of the future issues managers are considering as important. Issues that affect organizations can be either external or internal.

We have also illustrated, with three examples, what is already taking place within some organizations. These examples raise more questions for both the futurologists and the managers. They also tell us how careful futurologists ought to be. Indeed, the future they describe has a good chance of materializing: Their forecasts can be "self-fulfilling prophecies."

The postindustrial era described twenty years ago is at our doorstep, but it has taken an unexpected form. In a lot of instances it looks very premature — that is, the new era has started before we have had time to fully exploit the industrial era. Everyone has been so eager to reach "the paradise" that has been described that we may have accelerated the movement in that direction without fully realizing the conditions required for its existence.

CHAPTER 6

Management in the Next Thirty Years: Notes about Performance and Governance

WILLIAM R. DILL

As astrologers for the next thirty years, it helps to know sunspots from blind spots. We do live in a world of changing expectations that will push organizations and their managers in new directions. Some of our greatest problems, though, stem from disappointed expectations, from hopes about managerial intentions and promises that have not been fulfilled. Tomorrow's agenda is not all new. Much, though, is reconsideration of items that should have been handled better yesterday.

Consider the concept of change itself and the conclusion that we are living in especially turbulent times — in what Peter Drucker has called "the age of discontinuity." Many of the biggest changes with which we are trying to contend are changes for which strongly managed, activist organizations in society are largely responsible. Innovations in communication and transportation have helped create the circumstances that bind us in a combination of partnership and confrontation with the Third World. Successful stimulation of large appetites for consumption has aggravated environmental and resource problems, which now raise concerns for clean air and water and alternative supplies of energy. Affluence at levels for masses of citizens never before seen in human history has something to do with complaints that young Europeans and Americans do not share the stern work ethic of their parents. Vigorous work in the design and marketing of weaponry has given troubling new dimensions both to big-power politics and to local terrorism. Much of the so-called turbulence should be no more of a surprise to a thoughtful manager than backwash from a jet engine is to a skilled engineer.

Our fascination with change and turbulence also reflects the size of organizations that most of us represent and serve. Success, ambitions for growth and immortality, and supportive developments in the art and technology of management have made it possible for bigger organizational forms to emerge and thrive. Today's corporations and public enterprises are far beyond the scale imagined by Adam Smith or socialists a century or two ago. They are huge in the resources they command, in the complexity and diversity of tasks they undertake, and in the geographic dispersal of their operations. The best, like some of the major multinational corporations, are impressively focused and integrated worldwide systems.

Yet large organizations, like supertankers, cannot turn on a dime. Strategic planning for them has become a process not only of forecasting the environment and adapting to it, but of shaping the environment so that it will sustain their internal momentum. Smaller entities and individual citizens sometimes feel that the rules of the road have been rewritten — as they have indeed for small-boat sailors in the path of supertankers, so that they, not the large organization, are supposed to yield rights of way.

Our main challenge today, then, may not be to debate new

trends in the environment, since most of the important ones are amply visible to those who care to look and analyze. It may be, instead, to think through the design of large organizations and the preparation of their managers so that the environment will seem to boil forth with fewer sudden shocks.

General Motors did not need to be surprised by Ralph Nader or the energy crisis. American colleges and universities have no excuse for failing to read the market decline that population statistics foretold more than a decade in advance. The United States ought to have understood the inherent instabilities of political and social organization in Iran. Hopefully, Western firms in their current euphoria about new business with China are estimating some of the risks that exist for sudden reversals in power structure and orientation of the People's Republic. For all we may need to discuss changing expectations, we need even more to discuss how to make systems more alert to expectations, new and old, and more flexible and effective in their response.

It is tempting also to overestimate the degree to which organizations are being transformed to new missions and new goals. While there are clear pressures on old-line economic enterprises to show greater awareness of overall social responsibilities and to learn to live with more complex goal structures, the story of the next thirty years may be the degree to which other institutions in society are forced to sharpen their emphasis on traditional economic performance dimensions. We seem far more likely to create a *plus*-industrial than a *post*industrial society.

At the core of any private enterprise must remain discipline and selectivity in setting goals, efficiency in the marshaling and use of economic and human resources, and a dedication to short-term response — sales and return on capital — in the marketplace. Such performance variables figure centrally in urgent discussions today of how to improve the delivery of governmental services, the record of public enterprises in socialist countries, and the development of both private and public enterprise in developing nations. They also figure in the transition that some feel is overtaking us, from a product to a service-oriented economy. Such a transition is not a retreat from "industrialization," but as those involved with information and word processing systems know, a search for new patterns of efficient mass production based on computers and communications technology.

Because the most important decisions seem to come down to

who manages and how they account for their decisions, the years ahead are likely to be years of ferment about the governance of organizations. Partly this will be a continuation of long-term ideological debates about the organization of society. These debates are accentuated today because for the first time the whole variety of alternative approaches our world offers are in close practical interactions with one another. At the same time, they are accentuated because people are finding it less and less profitable to try to resolve twentieth- and twenty-first-century issues by reference to eighteenth- and nineteenth-century assumptions and arguments. Much of the governance ferment will be local, as institutions within a country debate new arrangements for such things as codetermination, financial disclosure, outside majorities for boards of directors. The dominant issues, though, are international ones and affect the oversight of both private and public organizations.

Governance of the Multinational Enterprise

The most troublesome issue is who governs the multinational enterprise. This is complex because such enterprises are big enough to dominate some of the countries with which they deal, dispersed enough to operate in parts of the world that have very different and often conflicting cultures and value systems, and independent enough sometimes to regard themselves as citizens of the world rather than as loyalists to their home countries. Even within large and powerful home countries, they can be shapers of foreign policy, not merely servants to it. Multinationals pose problems of governance both because, at times, they are properly seen as Colossus dominating the societies with which they deal and because, at other times, they can be described as Gulliver in Lilliput, rendered helpless by a tangle of threads tied by the conflicting jurisdictions in which they operate.

There are many questions. What role do the countries in which a multinational operates play in the selection and evaluation of the people who lead it as officers and directors? Within those countries where the government itself is not democratic or representative of the people's interests, how does a multinational firm establish a base of legitimacy with the citizenship itself? How reasonable is it for groups to use multinational firms as instruments for achieving change in another country (such as South Africa) in the absence of official governmental endorsement for the change? What supranational powers are being considered to guide or regulate multinationals? What kinds of institutions make sense to exercise such powers? What limits should apply to such powers with respect to the right of sovereign national governments? In different kinds of country environments, how can company disclosure and coverage of company operations by the mass media best be planned to build a base of informed public opinion for evaluation and criticism of a firm's performance? Where multiple jurisdictions, conflicting values, and pressures for local autonomy in oversight arrangements exist, how do we protect firms and their overall constituencies from excessive burdens of cost, confusion, and contradiction in regulation? It is hard to predict the outcomes, but we seem genuinely to be entering a period of search from which both new corporate and new governmental structures may emerge.

Outreach and Strategic Planning

Another worldwide governance issue concerns outsiders who have a stake in what an organization does. How do we involve them more actively and effectively in the process of making strategic plans rather than in simply judging results? Most structures for governance in Western countries have been results- rather than plan-oriented — first because planning has only recently become a visible and consequential organizational activity, and second because a results orientation is conservative in the restrictions that it places on an organization's initiative and autonomy. Now, however, strategic planning matters. Planning is one of management's most significant activities. It has developed with management's assuming it could do most of the job quite well itself, without outside help. And while it has produced many successes, it has also led organizations into some long-term commitments both they and society have come to regret.

How do we appropriately encourage or specify outreach in the course of developing goals and plans for an enterprise? While it may help to specify more diversified backgrounds for trustees or directors at the top of an organization, how do we assure arrangements for similarly direct flows of advice to professional and managerial groups at lower levels? Insensitivity to external conditions in putting plans together often starts with experts far down in an organization. Should we try to supplement and check the planning the organizations do by greater efforts at parallel research and analysis outside, as we do now with governmental efforts to generate economic forecasts and to assess new technology? Or should we rely more on adversarial reviews, such as environmental impact evaluations and, more generally, the current expansion of critical business journalism? Parallel research is a friendly and constructive process but is often disappointingly cozy and unproductive if the teams are working from similar and perhaps equally mistaken assumptions and approaches. Adversarial exchanges may bring out issues better, but they tend to encourage stridency and oversimplification on both sides and to lead to divisive and bitter outcomes.

Or, as we identify key questions and alternatives, should there be more emphasis on polling stakeholders about the choices they prefer? This is consistent with democratic ideals but threatening in what it implies for violation of the competitive secrecy enterprises maintain and dubious in terms of the quality of judgments many outsiders would make. Informed respondents must be able not only to understand and weigh factors that affect them directly, but also to look with restraint at trade-offs that should be made now in favor of future generations.

We need experience with voluntary experiments in public participation more than we need prescriptions, but it does seem clear that the more important and binding that planning efforts become, the more they inevitably will be subject to outside advice and review before they are confirmed and implemented. Such reviews cannot be allowed to destroy entrepreneurial willingness to take risks, and they must be bounded in the costs and time involved so that decisions do get made and organizations can move ahead.

Two Challenges for Management Education

Over the next thirty years the pressures for flexibility and performance, the ferment about governance, and other developments pose two major challenges for management education. The first is to come to terms with the reality that there is no single ideal management prototype to train, but rather a diverse family of managers and support professionals who all have important roles to play in tomorrow's organizations. The second is to help bring some of the things we emphasize with managers into the mainstream of general public education, worldwide.

In regard to the first challenge, management education has made its mark so far in preparing leaders and managers for economic performance: *operations managers*, with an eye for efficiency and a skill for delivering on complex goals and commitments; *support specialists* in technical fields such as control, operations analysis, finance, and personnel; and *strategic organizers and leaders*, good at goal-setting, design of incentives and performance-oriented systems, facilitation of resource flows, and measurement of results. We have been looking for ways, also, to develop creative and innovative skills and to expand the pool of *entrepreneurial talent* — some out on its own, some within large organizations — whose gift is for conceiving and launching new enterprises.

We are concerned now with orienting men and women with these general credentials for productive work in new environments: in tightening direction and improving efficiency for governmental and other not-for-profit organizations and in adapting approaches that have worked in product-oriented settings to meet the expanding prominence of service industries.

Further, though, there must be emphasis on creating several new categories of talent to deal with the political fortunes of organizations as they wrestle with problems of governance and seek to anchor their place and role in society. One kind is the *politician-statesmen*, individuals who will often find their way to the chief executive's spot, who are able to be good listeners, strong advocates and shapers of policy, and credible participants in public as well as private decision-making. Another category, perhaps to be prepared after experience in other roles, is the *trustee*, the overseer or director who has a responsibility to bring outside perspectives and skills in questioning and in judgment to the board room. Still another category is *support professionals*, those who have skills as *communicators* in helping managers develop approaches for hearing from and dealing with outside constituencies and those who have skills as *negotiators* in bargaining with governments and with particular stakeholder constituencies.

No one individual is likely to master all the roles, and no one educational center is likely to serve all of them well. A greater degree of coordination will be required of organizations, governments, universities, and independent centers to make sure that the whole family of needs is being met.

The second challenge stems from the fact that we have let the world become dependent on economic, technological, and organizational processes that it only vaguely understands. Our managerial success in making the world a single economy puts great pressure on us to help different peoples to understand one another. Levels of public education generally are grossly inadequate for assuring understanding either of modern organizations or of deeply rooted historical and cultural traditions. Managers and their organizations need a better base of education in society to help build and maintain credibility with various publics. Credibility requires in basic terms an understanding and acceptance of what we have tried to build. That educational task is one we too long have left to others and one in which managers and management educators should now play a larger part.

PART II

Management in the XXI Century

CHAPTER 7

Retrospects and Prospects

BORIS YAVITZ

This part of the book will focus on three dimensions of managerial work in the twenty-first century:

1. Role and function;
2. Authority and responsibility;
3. Satisfaction and self-perception.

Because each of the foregoing will be affected by the major societal trends earlier identified, I deem it wise to note the principal sections of the earlier commentary that impact most directly on each of the three dimensions of management. A few key points or issues are highlighted under each section.

Role and Function of the Manager

Of the various trends that suggest a change in *what* managers of the future will be doing and *how* they will be doing it, the trends mentioned below seem particularly relevant.

Availability, scarcity, and rising costs of raw materials and energy are likely to affect managerial roles in a number of areas:

- Strategic planning — new approaches to identifying opportunities and threats, competition, and collaboration;
- Different dimensions for allocating and computing capital investments, earning streams, and risks;
- Introduction of new or unfamiliar technologies as a means of developing substitutions and alternate sources;
- Means of dealing with conservation programs, both voluntary and legislated;
- More complex decision-making through consideration of trade-offs between costs, ecology, safety, efficiency, quality, and so forth.

The changing international order and its implications to international business and trade raise a number of key issues:

- The role of the multinational corporation in world trade and the attitudes of national governments to it and its executives;
- The degree to which managers will become directly involved in political and diplomatic negotiations for materials, energy, and technology transfers;
- Increasing pressures for adaptation to many varied cultures and the understanding of diverse national aspirations.

Changing values and social beliefs raise some key questions about the basic role of the manager:

- A social/political entrepreneur or an economic optimizer;
- An agent of growth or contraction, stability or change;
- A designer and implementer of multidimensional cost/benefit analyses and criteria.

How are all these developments likely to affect managerial roles and functions? And, going a step further, what are the skills, technical competences, and bodies of knowledge that need to be mastered?

Authority, Responsibility, and Legitimacy of Management

Here we are concerned with attempting to define the parameters of responsibility and authority imposed on managers and the governance system within which they will operate. Simply put, *to whom* will managers be responsible? And *for what?* Where will their authority come from? And how will they exercise it? Three major trends seem of particular interest.

Changing institutions in society and the interrelationships between them can be expected to affect issues of governance and responsibility:

- Growing public skepticism toward traditional institutions;
- Complex relationships between the public, "semipublic," and private sectors; the seeming paradox of societies calling for more government intervention at the same time that they become more critical of its performance; the question of how much can/ should be left to market mechanisms;
- The varied, conflicting, and increasingly more demanding (and more politically active) constituencies of private and public organizations — an issue illustrated by current debates on the composition and representation of boards of directors;
- The growing number of institutions constraining or conflicting with managerial authority (e.g., labor unions, professional associations, foreign governments, local community boards, and so forth).

Changing values encompass many dimensions; several of these, however, have direct bearing on managerial authority and its exercise:

- A perceived trend of declining acceptance of hierarchical au-

thority; a growing demand for individual participation in decision-making and increasing emphasis on equality;

- Growing concern for noneconomic, societal goals may constrain
  management's authority and power, suggesting new dimensions
  in "social responsibility" and "corporate legitimacy";
- A series of dynamic shifts in balance of power between individuals, organizations, national governments, and international
  institutions.

*Science, technology, and production have an impact on orga-
nizations that goes far beyond determining their mechanical processes. Advances in science and technology will also affect:*

- The political and governing structure of the organization — how
  much centralization or decentralization of authority is feasible
  and desirable, the advantages of size, of backward integration
  of services over products, and so on;
- The degree of flexibility or rigidity of the production process
  and its impact on worker satisfaction, on potential for growth,
  and on organizational stability;
- The possibility of extended social or governmental controls over
  science and technology applications, which could take the form
  of regulation of production processes as well as interventions
  in international transfers of technology; it should also be noted
  that the extension of controls may well be accelerated by another trend — vulnerability of complex societies to disruption
  of increasingly interdependent and "brittle" technologies.

Are all these trends likely to make significant differences in the
responsibilities societies will place on their organizations? The authority they will delegate to their managers? And the constituencies
to which they will be accountable?

Motivation, Satisfaction, and Morale of the Manager

The way in which managers behave will depend, in great part, on
the way in which they perceive themselves and their function. The
commitment to their job — and the vigor with which they pursue
it — will depend on the satisfaction and motivation they will find

in managing. A number of trends will help shape managerial self-perceptions, inspirations, and rewards.

Changing values raise a number of important questions:

- Are individual, personal goals shifting (from things that are primarily material/economic) toward greater emphasis on intangible/social values?
- Is the traditional "work ethic" fading? What values are replacing it? Do they differ markedly in different cultures? Is work seen as a vehicle for mobility, advancement, self-fulfillment, or simply a means of economic survival?
- Is there a shift in the loyalty and commitment individuals believe they owe to their organization, profession, family, social group, or nation?
- What are the implications for individuals of living with uncertainty and ambiguity as the daily reality of professional life?

The changing international order adds a number of extra dimensions to the questions raised above:

- Will differing societal expectations around the world lead to significantly different self-perceptions and reward structures for managers? If so, which will have primary impact on the "international" manager?
- Differing expectations will also lead to differing criteria of managerial "success" and performance measurement. Will such traditional values as growth and efficiency decline in importance?
- Will the large, multinational corporations emerge as new arenas for personal growth and development, or as constraining, initiative-stifling bureaucracies?

Classes and groups of people pose questions of further differentiation in the identity and motivation of managers:

- Does the growing number of working wives or two-income families portend rapid acceleration in numbers of women managers; radical change in traditional family roles and constraints on travel, job changes, relocations; different level of acceptance of male and female authority by subordinates and superiors?

- Is the younger, better-educated manager likely to follow a career path quite different from those we are currently accustomed to?
- Will the aging populations and the changing attitudes toward retirement in the industrially advanced nations lead to shorter or longer managerial life spans? Or to earlier retirements and increased mobility opportunities within an organization? Or to postponed retirement with fewer openings and slower rates of advancement?

The answers to these questions will help assess a number of important issues: Will there be a sufficient supply of managers to meet society's needs? Where will they come from, and what will be their outstanding personal characteristics? What values and incentives will be motivating them to take on the challenging tasks ahead? And will their careers vary markedly from present norms?

Lest we tend to underestimate the importance of this undertaking, let me note two things. First, the lead-time we necessarily deal with is measured in decades, not years. The senior executives of the major organizations in the year 2000 have already graduated from their respective universities. It is quite appropriate for us to be concerned with the twenty-first century now. Second, there is not a single, preordained future that must inevitably prevail. Rather, the future we face will depend in large part on the actions we take (or fail to take) today and tomorrow. In this sense our concern is not simply with managers *for* the future, but also managers *of* the future.

This activity then, is not an esoteric, theoretical exercise but an urgent and highly practical one. The effectiveness with which our society will select, educate, and develop its future managers will largely determine the quality and richness of the lives of our children and grandchildren.

CHAPTER 8

For the Manager, the Future Is Now

FLETCHER BYROM

When we are talking about what the manager is going to be thirty years from now, I submit that most of the things described in this book already exist today. This effort should probably have taken place a quarter-century ago! That explains why I have chosen to do what I am going to do in discussing the role and function of management. Initially, I thought of spelling out in great detail the functions of the chief executive officer, which include everything one could possibly ascribe to somebody in terms of responsibility. I could then conclude by saying cryptically that is what it is today.

The critical question for educators is how to work out a curriculum that will prepare managers. However, I really don't think I have any right to try to speak as though I have some eternal wisdom about the function of the manager. Probably the most honest thing to do is to describe what we are trying to do presently in the Koppers Company, because that, in fact, tells you what I believe ought to be done. If it is not what ought to be done, then I ought to be kicked out of the company for doing what we are doing. Basically we instituted, in the early 1960s, what we thought was a very sophisticated planning effort that used all the modern techniques available in trying to understand the nature of society and the influences on our corporation ten years away. What we have learned is that our ability to project such things is probably within a two-year time frame at the most. About all you can get from a very quantitative, sophisticated approach to planning is a recognition that things will not turn out the way you expected them to. This recognition caused us to change our whole approach. Fundamentally, we decided that the standard rules of organizational practice that have been accepted (and still are accepted in many places) just do not fit today — and they certainly will not fit twenty years from now.

My early predecessor in the Koppers Company ran the firm on the theory that all managers are replaceable; therefore, there should be, in the well-ordered organizational structure, no irreplaceable individual. The system of job descriptions, limits of authority, organizational charts, procedural manuals, and the like would insure that the individuals in a particular job at a particular time would perform that function in the same way their predecessors did and in the same way their successors would. It was strictly a military orientation. The fact that it was General Sommerville who followed this orientation might lend some reason to it.

Fundamentally, we still have, in much of industrial organization, a pyramidal kind of framework with line and staff concepts based on military systems. An incident illustrates my point. Not too long ago I was invited to speak to the Kraft Company management on style and management philosophy. As it happened, I followed Walter Menninger, from the Menninger Clinic, who spoke on how to remove stress in the management job. By the time he completed his remarks, I was embarrassed about getting up and following him. Why? Because, essentially, everything Dr. Menninger said should not be done we deliberately do at Koppers. Why we do what we do can be simply stated and economically justified.

We do not believe that a rigidly structured organization, bureaucratic in nature, can successfully deal with the environment in which we operate now and shall operate during the next twenty or thirty years. Interestingly enough, a study was completed some ten years ago (based on Maslovian hierarchy of needs) where the investigators were talking about American values in the 1990s. The conclusion I remember is this: As affluence of society changed, individuals would be motivated less by money incentives and more by goals of self-actualization. Willis Harmon has done work wherein he ascribes to corporations the responsibility for developing self-definition as the principal objective of the job description in an organization. Frankly, some years ago we at Koppers came to the conclusion that this is where we were headed and we had better get on with it. Peter McCulloch of Xerox said that the organization of the future would be one that is able to assign responsibility for decision-making at the level closest to where the greatest impact of the decision will be felt.

Fundamentally, the whole thrust of organizational practice in our company today is to disaggregate the corporation as rapidly as we can into complete entities where the person in charge will, in fact, have essentially the same authority as the CEO. By that we mean that this person must have skill in community relations; possess a public presence, the ability to negotiate contracts, a sense of responsibility toward the environment and affirmative action plans; and be responsible for occupational safety. You name it — these managers do it. Basically, what Koppers does is to take people who have employable skills (shown by a specialty in engineering, accounting, or whatever) and assume that those who move to successful leadership in our company will be those who proceed to broaden themselves as rapidly as they can in as many other disciplines as is possible — and other than the one in which they have received their formal training.

We firmly believe that anyone who is not willing to proceed on this basis is not going to be a major contributor to our operation. How do we translate belief into practice? Let me illustrate. Koppers negotiates all of its labor contracts at the plant level. We have 278 operation locations, and I suppose we have about 260 of them unionized. We also hold the plant manager responsible for that plant's community relationships. For example, in California we have an operation where, every time there will be a change that alters the noise level (or gives some kind of effluent different from past patterns), the plant manager, who has already organized the residential community around him under block leaders, brings these block leaders in for a day's indoctrination on what is going on and what is contemplated. The leaders go back to advise the community: When there is a bleep where there used to be a blop, the community will not become agitated about the change. This manager did this on his own initiative. We have now taken that example and said to everyone: "You characters had better start doing this." The point is that the whole thrust of our attitude toward operations is that, increasingly, we want to disaggregate the organization into smaller and smaller pieces. It has to be done with a centralized kind of sensing system, so that we are fundamentally operating on an after-the-fact management style. Initiatives are taken, and successful ones are built into the system.

The implication for education, so far as I am concerned, is not that educators must turn out a finished product. We want you to give us, not a piece of rock, but, rather, a piece of fertile ground upon which additional seeds of knowledge can be sown effectively. We are perfectly willing to accept the responsibility for serving as sowers of seeds. Basically, our system of delegation is that anyone responsible for anything within the framework of his or her responsibility has my full authority and, in effect, can speak for me, recognizing that he or she would have to explain to me the reasonableness of the decision to act in this way. Managers do not have to be right; nor must they do it as I would do it. But they must have a rationale for their actions. This means that managers must possess a broad enough knowledge base to make a conclusion as to what would be a rational action. We are literally talking about a person for all seasons; we are looking for people capable of taking the *complete* responsibility for what they are doing within the framework of their responsibility. The only limitation, as we see it, is not in terms of the breadth of responsibility but the focus of the particular assignment. For example, where we had five divisions a year and a half ago, we now have fifty. Where we had one president, we now have five. Our staff reports to all five presidents. People ask how a staff can report to five presidents. The answer comes best in an incident. Recently, I was talking to one of our staff department managers who said: "I have more responsibility now than ever before; whereas in the past the president knew what he wanted from me, today when I have a good rationale of what to do, I am able to get three out of the five presidents to go along with me. And the other two then argue about it." Clearly, he was having a much bigger impact than he had as a young man, when there was only one individual he reported to.

In summary, the whole thrust of our operation is increasingly to provide self-definition for individuals in their jobs; what that means when you move to higher and higher levels of educational achievements is that everybody wants my job. In the typical structure, everybody cannot have my job. If, however, we change the nature of the organizational structure to the point where there are a hundred people who can have it, they are going to be happy for a long time. I think this is possible. I further think that when it happens, we shall have destroyed the tendency toward rigidity that comes from a bureaucratic, pyramidal structure. My point is that this is already happening. My view of what you have to be training for — and should have been training for during the last thirty years — is a kind of management responsibility where, at every level of the organization, there is a maximization of the individual's potential. We must give a totality of responsibility to a specific job. I grant that not everybody is going to agree with this proposition. Frankly, I am very happy that they do not because, as they stick to the old structure of operating, we shall run circles around them!

CHAPTER 9

Legitimacy, Management Authority, and Corporate Governance: A Comparative View

NEIL CHAMBERLAIN

Throughout the postwar period, and increasingly in the last decade, there have emerged in the industrialized countries sets of problems that are proving obdurate. The catalogue is depressingly familiar: unemployment; inflation; scarcity of and control over resources, especially energy; concern over deterioration of the natural environment, the civic environment, and the working environment; impatience with traditional forms of hierarchical authority and demands for more extensive participation in economic decision-making, both public and private; problems of linking domestic economies with a changing set of international relations.

The European and American responses to these problems have differed. The responses by political parties within Western Europe and within North America have likewise differed. But the problems remain the same. Shifts in ideological thinking from one government to the next may affect short-run approaches but not the need for long-run adjustments. In my view, regardless of political auspices, the result will be to modify the basis of management's authority and the degree of corporate autonomy. First, with respect to Western Europe, both management and the corporation are the object of a pincers movement. The intractable economics and related problems cannot be resolved by reliance on an unstructured free market. Governments of all persuasions have had to identify social objectives and seek instruments for realizing them. When indicative planning — an instrument for "rationalizing" the existing institutional framework, largely conceived by technocrats and industrialists — failed to realize its promise, it was succeeded by industrial policy and selective intervention. When rising unemployment reinforced the need for effective international competition, government intervention in support of technologically advanced industries was joined by government rescue operations for traditional industries ranging from textiles to shipbuilding. Similarly, labor market policy moved away from general measures emphasizing mobility and training to selective measures designed for employment security.

Despite recent shifts in governments and the political philosophies characterizing them, there seems little prospect of abandoning some industrial policy and selective intervention in response to specific pressures and national needs. Indeed, the likelihood would seem to be to attempt to make such policy more coherent and consistent rather than piecemeal and ad hoc. This may signal some future — perhaps imminent — effort at combining planning and industrial policy. In any event, the result will be to impose on corporate autonomy and management discretion the guiding hand of government, not out of ideological persuasion but out of political responsibility. This is one arm of the pincers movement.

The other arm of the pincers comes from the labor unions. Since 1968 national organizations have been prodded by the rank-and-file to take a more active role in structuring the work environment and operating decisions affecting working conditions. Legislation has given structure to this spontaneous movement — notably, the German law of 1972 and the Swedish law of 1976. In addition, national union leaders (not without exceptions) have pushed for continuing representation in corporate decision-making at the board level, a movement that has been given support by the so-called Fifth Directive of the European Community. The present significance of board representation is more open to question than is the significance of worker participation at the operating level, but there are substantial reasons to believe that the former will acquire more meaning in time. It would seem reasonable to conclude that managers in the future will have to share some portion of their authority with worker representatives on a range of matters from occupational safety to plant closure, from technical procedures to the location of investment.

If management decision-making and corporate policy are to be more responsive to political pressures both from government and labor, this will necessitate some "breathing space" for the rigors of an unregulated international competition. The need to insure international competitiveness for national survival has served as a discipline both on government policy and labor union bargaining. If the competitive free market is subjected to some measured constraint, that discipline is relaxed and the play of political decision is readmitted. In any event, pressures from the volatile non-Western world are already emphasizing that negotiation, at least as much as competition, will be the basis for future international economic relations. The consequence will be a need for Western powers to rethink their own internal political decision-making procedures to incorporate those organizations, especially corporations and unions, whose actions can importantly affect outcomes. If management loses independent discretion in some respect, it may thus gain influence over wider areas of decision-making having to do with public policy.

The situation in North America is somewhat different. The United States and Canada are subject to many, if not most, of the same pressing problems confronting Western Europe. Their traditions and institutions differ, however. American labor unions lack the political identity labor unions have in Europe. They have been less concerned with issues and more concerned with economic reward. On the other hand, American managements — despite their reputation as free-market hard-liners — have been more public relations–minded. Instead of rejecting social responsibility, they have, for the most part, sought to define it in a way that both disarms their critics and preserves their discretion. Where this has failed, the gap has been filled by selective government intervention of a regulatory nature. One of the most significant aspects of the impressive body of regulatory legislation is that, realistically, it is enforceable only through the voluntary compliance of the companies regulated. Government budgets and manpower do not permit any broad-scale enforcement; they are largely restricted to precedent-making or symbolic actions. Corporate good faith must supply the principal enforcer.

The general attitude of public skepticism toward the exercise of authority has not, however, bypassed the corporation. Although managerial concern for public relations has curbed some of the worst excesses of business, there is a continuing, probably growing, belief among nonbusiness and even some business leaders that corporations, as self-interest groups, cannot be entrusted with the public interest; some check on their continuing performance is needed. My judgment is that in the United States it is not likely to come from a more pervasive governmental intervention or from labor union involvement — the pincers movement of Europe. It is more likely to come through constituting the outside directors, who now compose a majority on most of the large corporation boards, into some form of public directors, with a broadened mandate to serve a larger, if amorphous, constituency.

If these observations have even a modicum of validity, they lead to several conclusions:

- Managerial competence, both in Western Europe and North America, must extend to political (as much as economic or technocratic) expertise. Training for managers cannot be so narrowly conceived as a specialization that it excludes fundamental concern and intellectual aptitudes for political and social issues of the broadest nature.

- The approach to decision-making, while it cannot do without some role for authority, must rest more heavily on effecting agreement through compromise. The notion of a right or rational answer to most of the significant problems will be less and less tenable.

- What is involved is not simply changing roles and institutions of business, but of all major groups, especially government and labor. If the free competitive market is no longer so generally applicable, neither is free collective bargaining. Some form of an incomes policy appears to be essential. If a different social and economic strategy dictates a modified and accommodating corporate structure, the same is likely to be true of government structure. Some more effective form of functional participation must be accommodated within a representative system.

CHAPTER 10

Management Motivation in the XXI Century

FRANS VAN DEN HOVEN

Setting the Scene

People's needs, values, and expectations change with the conditions around them. What will remain crucial at all times is that "managing" will always be a human activity and thus ultimately influenced by the interplay of human forces.

Management motivation, satisfaction, and morale by the year 2010 will be determined not only by the social, economic, and political environment for business at that time, but also very much by the trends and developments in the era between now and the turn of the century. Indeed, the middle/top managers in the early part of the next century, already have, on the whole, been born.

Many are in advanced stages of education and are very much aware of the world around them. They are in the formative stage of their development, and by the turn of the century, their behavior will therefore be heavily influenced by their own experiences in the next decades and by the philosophy and behavior of their present tutors. So in discussing the manager's motivation, satisfaction, need, and morale in the new century, we must take account of both the pertinent factors determining the business conditions by 2010 and the main relevant "shaping" trends and issues (now and in the years to come) that may have lasting imprint on the manager's future behavior.

Elements Relevant to Management Behavior in Early Twenty-First-Century Society

Earlier sections of this volume have dealt with the evolutionary forces producing both change and changing expectations in the various societies over the next thirty years. Several visions of the future have been presented; each provides a different setting for management behavior and motivation by the year 2010. Apart from these various future views on a global basis, the first part of this book analyzes the different developments between the industrialized and the developing world. In the first group of countries, the changes are mainly sociopolitical in nature; in the second, transformations are chiefly concerned with raising the standard of living. But even within each group we perceive large differences — for example, in the developed world sharp differentiations are manifest among Japan, the United Kingdom, Germany, and North America. These differences need not necessarily narrow in the future; on the contrary, they may widen. In the developing countries the pace and direction of change will also show large variations, depending on such matters as the political and religious systems, the availability of energy and other resources, and literacy levels.

Bringing too many assumptions into play overcomplicates the issues; therefore, we must realize that the environment for each manager in a particular country will be at a different state of development. While it is tempting to forecast a continuation of the present trends, this would disregard the self-corrective capabilities of societies forced by changing values or by simple economic realities. Consequently, we may well see a return to some values of the past.

However, certain trends will continue. We shall live in an increasingly international world and, at the same time, in a more open world; the corporation will be more transparent so that influences from the outside will be felt more keenly. Therefore, the interaction between business and its environment will be greater. For the large multinational corporation this will happen both on a national and on an international scale. In turn, managers — especially top managers — will become more aware that they have a critical role to play in shaping the environment as it affects business. Inside the corporation there will be a continuous, growing need for relevant information and genuine consultation in the area that affects the individual employee's work. In general, it will mean greater involvement by people at various levels in running the business.

In the industrialized world the changing age pattern will cause important shifts in market demand. Fewer young people will enter the labor market, and there will be more competition for good management. Unemployment could be easing off in spite of the West's becoming a more highly technological society. This will be a world where people, with the exception of those in various underdeveloped countries, will have all the material needs to survive and prosper. Having fulfilled that basic need, motivation will turn more heavily in the direction of quality of life, dignity, and self-fulfillment. The greatest problem is to learn to live together and to find meaning living in a society with less individual freedom. Self-fulfillment will, more than at present, be derived from one's contribution to the society at large. In the West we will continue to live in a market economy, although there may be more state enterprise and much more regulation. Trade unions may well find it more important to try to influence the political scene, at least in Western Europe. Competition will continue to be the cornerstone in our economies on both an international and a national scale. The more advanced developing countries, with modern industries and relatively cheap labor, will become an important competitive factor in certain sectors of the world economy.

These are some of the major trends that will affect the manager's outlook, decision-making, and motivation. However, the challenge to business will be even greater. In what follows, I shall look rather quickly at three broad areas (changing values, political-economic factors, and social environment) and suggest how each will possibly influence the manager's motivations.

A Different Set of Values for Business

Individual and group well-being will undoubtedly remain an important goal; however, in the industrialized world there will be less emphasis on material goods and more emphasis on quality of work, leisure, the environment, and interhuman relationships. In such a situation growth does remain an important target, although in a different overall setting of priorities, and it is much harder to achieve because of growing constraints and conflicting demands. But growth will continue to be a prerequisite for the continuity of each enterprise. Moreover, it will also be the only means to go on fulfilling the needs of people and to improve the quality of life.

Parallel to the evolution in the human needs, growth in business terms will no longer be confined to growth in terms of volume and profit alone. A return on investment or profit will remain the main measurement of ensuring the continuity of the enterprise. But the true value of this measurement may well be the enterprise's simultaneous ability to meet new demands by society. Private enterprise will still be the innovator and, as such, the creator of wealth. But its role as a responsible member of the community will become an equally important *raison d'etre*.

This means that business will become "yet another" body in society that must prove its usefulness. Recognition of this role by the outside world will be an important factor in management motivation. Individual shareholders may well have been replaced by institutional holdings in which public and semipublic partnerships will play a large role. They will develop a similar outlook as the management of the enterprise. Exceptions to this overall pattern will be the very small privately owned businesses operating at the periphery of the then highly regulated Western world.

POSSIBLE IMPACT ON MOTIVATION

Profit achievement, while at the same time fulfilling the other demands of society, will be the greatest challenge to managers. Job satisfaction for managers will be influenced by their status in the community, since a broader-based activity will be the way to reach satisfaction and status once material well-being has been secured. Achievement as a motivational force will therefore become more diffuse and will depend on a multitude of operational goals partly related to the sociopolitical environment. This will work out very differently from person to person. Association with a successful business will change. The greatest problem in terms of motivational clarity will be for managers and their superiors to pinpoint the proper goals — what are the appropriate targets, their priorities, and their limits.

Politics, Economics, and Prosperity

POLITICS

In the name of protecting the individual, the trend to restrict individual freedom will continue. By the turn of the century, governments both national and international will have set very detailed rules for business in terms of product, environment, and community behavior. In Northern Europe the emphasis may continue to be in the social-political area, while in the United States the influence of the regulatory agencies will be more and more felt. In some countries this may produce a backlash in the long term. Internationally, the Western world will have to come to terms with the developing countries on some of the major issues, although what is termed the "New Economic Order" may be a long way off.

Power in the multinational business world will also be much more "evenly" distributed and subject to more rules and regulations. Apart from direct government intervention, many more groups than at present will emerge with vested interests, thereby making the society rigid and subject to veto groupings. Collective groups (outside and inside the business) will try to alter the rules of the game. These will be competitive, and the society may become dominated by a battle of intellects. Legitimacy through strong leadership will fade. In order to keep society manageable there will also be strong tendencies toward decentralization — with detailed local rulings often in contradiction with central guidelines.

ECONOMICS AND PROSPERITY

Individual prosperity in the Western world will be very high compared to today's standards — even if growth in the next decades is moderate. In some of the more socially advanced countries, this question will have to be faced: Can the economy continue to support the welfare and regulatory programs? The impact on cost from the bureaucracy and from the change in moral values ("the state owes me a living") of an increasing number of people will be dramatic over a period of thirty years unless the tide is turned, *and this may well be the most crucial question to be faced.* In the developing countries there will be a growing awareness of the threat of population growth, as there will be little change from the present growth rates. Large parts of the populations will remain outside the cash economy, in spite of an "average" rise in living standards and enough basic foodstuffs grown. A number of moderately developed countries will make rapid progress and thus provide at least partial solutions to these problems. These countries may slowly reduce the gap with the industrialized world in wealth and know-how, but for all others the gap will tend to widen.

Energy supply may not be a major problem, albeit relatively more expensive, thanks to new inventions and improved use of existing resources (e.g., automation in coal mining). There will be no problem in the supply of raw materials, but the political price will be much higher.

POSSIBLE IMPACT ON MOTIVATION

This situation (with greatly reduced individual freedom of decision) will have a significant impact on the attitude of managers and on their motivation. Their environment will substantially influence what can and should be done. The room to make changes in this legalistic society will narrow. Under these circumstances the need for managers with initiative, drive, good political antennae, and entrepreneurial spirit will be greater than ever. But different kinds of persons may be attracted into organized business — that is, those who like to work within the system, go for the security of the rule book with a lawyer at their side, and prefer to belong to a vested institution. This will be accentuated by the high individual prosperity that will dampen the need to achieve in today's "narrow" business sense.

This changing environment could distract the scarce entrepreneurial types who want to achieve by setting their own goals and making their own decisions. They may well choose to go for their own private, very small setup to escape the rigid system network. Those who look for sheer power as their main motivator may turn their backs to business to join civil service and institutionalized pressure groups.

In developing countries there will be clear differences in motivation between managers in the various geographical areas. Perhaps the developing countries will "supply" the world with many more people with entrepreneurial drive than Europe and North America!

Social Environment: The Main Impact on Motivation

The greatest impact on management's behavior in the early part of the next century will be the fundamentally different social circumstances. Changes will be apparent in a number of areas.

POPULATION

The population will have stabilized or will be decreasing in the Western world. This means fewer young people, a dominating cluster of thirty-to-fifty-five-year-olds, and a large reservoir of retired people. The young will be in demand; the older groups may feel unwanted. Family ties will be loose, and very few men will be sole providers.

EMPLOYMENT

Employment, in terms of "job activity" in the Western world, will not be a problem by 2010. Jobs will perhaps not be greater in number as compared with the 1980s; on the other hand, labor supply will be sharply reduced because of decreasing population, more flexible retirement, a shorter working week, longer holidays, and fewer young entrants into the labor market. Feelings of insecurity in this respect will fade away. Social pressure against technological developments will gradually disappear. In the rest of the world, however, employment will still be a problem, and many will continue to seek work in the developed world, including work at the managerial level.

EDUCATION

The average level of education will not only be high but also much more evenly spread among people. Education will go afield — into the homes through electronic media, into union offices, factories, and so forth — and will reach all people of all ages. Know-how will, however, quickly become obsolete and the inspiration to go on learning will be more important than knowledge itself. Education will be adapted to this as the middle-age group grows; long periods of learning before going to work will be changed to a flexible learning/work mix. It will be important, by then, to blur the sharp separation between "work" and "learning." People's inherent urge for self-development and creativity should, therefore, be constantly motivated.

ORGANIZATION STRUCTURE

The human relationships at the workplace will have changed. Hierarchy in today's terms will vanish. Authority will depend on competence. Changing and temporary managerial task groups will have different leaders, depending on the goals set. Organizations will be unstructured and flat, flexible, and decentralized. Small units will be the basis and will work at home or in remote workplaces. This will be made possible by sophisticated electronic communication networks. There will be much more freedom to design one's own task. Coordination will become a major headache, and top management will be swamped by human communications problems. Participation will not be the issue anymore. Complex and decentralized structures will, however, have made the individual participation impact low.

REWARDS

Notwithstanding the fact that prosperity in Europe and North America will be high, even higher material gain will still remain an individual goal. It is questionable whether there will still be bonus payments solely geared to the profit improvement of the company. The emphasis on remuneration will be among the "scarcity" groups like young employees and those with a low level of skill; indeed, the average level of education will be so high that there will be very few unskilled people left. Income differentiation on the basis of scarcity will, to a certain extent, have come in place of some erosion of income differentials for sociopolitical purposes. This will be stronger in Western Europe than in the United States.

POSSIBLE IMPACT ON MOTIVATION

The social environment of work in the early part of the next century will have quite an impact on human behavior. Positive will be the effect on work and work conditions, both materially and in terms of mental challenge. The average quality of jobs will be high. Managers, working in small units and task teams, will gain a feeling of independence and self-development. The possibilities for self-expression and motivation will, however, no longer be bound to the job; indeed there will be many other "competing" activities, one of which will be the need for constant training. Reward and the potential for advancement will still be powerful motivators. A demotivating effect could come from income policies and taxations in certain countries.

In many respects the situation in the developing world will be much more "traditionally twentieth century," particularly at the managerial level. There will still be an acute need to get things accomplished, and the potential sense of achievement will be high. Many of the now underdeveloped countries will, by then, have a much more motivating environment in terms of entrepreneurial drive and behavior than the Western world.

Some Final Observations

The conditions in thirty years' time — and the factors influencing the future managers' long-term behavior — are complex, often contradictory, and difficult to assess in detail. Human ability to adapt is strong. However, behavioral reactions to all these input factors are unpredictable — even for the best of social scientists, let alone for a modest businessman! The best way to proceed would perhaps be an exchange of thought around some relevant questions against the background emerging from the trends just described.

In terms of needs and expectations, the manager in the early 2000s will be motivated by very attractive work conditions and interesting jobs. There will be less strict hierarchies; structures will be flexible and far-reaching; decentralization will give room for self-development, freedom to shape one's task, and leadership by competence. Job security for those in middle management and top jobs will be excellent. The young will be in demand, and will find many interesting positions available. There will be freedom and opportunity to move into occupations. The possibilities for individual "multisided development," in and outside the actual job, will be great. Commitment through participation will have been achieved, and this will give some sense of belonging. Material well-being will be high and will add to people's room to experiment in life. Many of these positive points will be less pronounced in the world outside Europe and North America, but an increasing number of countries in the Third World will rapidly move in the same direction. The still somewhat less "secure" circumstances in those areas will have the added advantage of motivating many more people to reach higher levels of prosperity by business achievement.

Against these positive aspects of motivation and human expectations are some negative consequences. The world by 2010 will have become very much more complex; it will be difficult to see the woods through the trees of rules and regulations. Managers shall have to adapt constantly — without, however, always quite understanding why and in what direction. They may experience a lack of guidance and could well be puzzled by confusion over who is in charge. Complex organizations and the need to decentralize will make individual contacts more difficult to maintain, and many will feel "left alone."

Achievement and human recognition will be hard to win, and there is the danger of lack of direction; what is expected? High expectations aroused during education may not always come true. Too much free time may lead people to look for achievement "elsewhere," but boredom may often be the result. Money will be taken for granted; and although people will go on striving for more, money will satisfy less. Self-image may therefore be in danger. The experience of those who remember the eighties and the early nineties will add to some of the feelings of pessimism, insecurity, alienation, and inadequacy.

CHAPTER 11

Management in the XXI Century

CLARENCE C. WALTON

Unlike the opening comments in this book, characterized by a series of interesting questions, this chapter provides an overview stated in the form of affirmations.

There are three major parts to this chapter:

1. What are the likely major constraints on managers in the future?

2. What are managers actually doing today to meet the demands and pressures of those constraints?

3. What *should* managers be doing over the next thirty years to deal effectively with problems of function, legitimacy, and morale?

Major Constraints on Managers of the Future

Confronted by currently visible changes in the world's society and by likely momentous future changes whose contours are quite unclear, we are acutely aware of what the late J. Robert Oppenheimer once called the "Law of Maximum Surprise." Oppenheimer was referring to those discontinuities in the progress of science that suddenly appeared — Newtonian physics, Einstein's theory of relativity, and the like. In the presence of puzzles and paradoxes, continuity and discontinuity, Oppenheimer's observation has relevance to this enterprise.

Nevertheless, heed should be given to this insight from the Talmud: "If you know not where you are going, any road will take you there." It is an obligation shared equally by practitioners and scholars to seek understanding of what societies will demand of managers of major organizations so that, through such understanding, managers can be more responsive to human needs. In this context we have identified three distinct features on the road map to the future: (1) coming demands on management, (2) available resources to meet those demands, and (3) the environment in which managers will perform.

THE DEMAND SIDE

1. Managers must satisfy two demands, not always compatible, that are being simultaneously made upon them: increases in living standards (wealth creation, job opportunities, and so on), and improvements in the quality of life (job satisfaction, personal creativity, and so on). The tension likely to be created by these twin demands will in no way ease societal pressures on managers for effective performance.

2. The developing nations will press more urgently for a redistribution of wealth and a redistribution of wealth-creating techniques.

3. Future boards of directors will demand more of the management team. Because the old notion of the CEO as the power figure will end, the manager will be less a power-wielder and more a power-broker.

4. Visibility of managerial goal-setting and operation (through

greater openness and disclosure) will become the accepted way of corporate life.

THE SUPPLY SIDE

1. While wide variations exist in different countries, the changing composition of populations may mean a decline in supply of fully talented and motivated people. The revolution in woman power makes predictions very vulnerable. On balance, however, the availability of managers will probably be strained.

2. Relative to the total sum of knowledge, which increases dramatically, will be a declining level in basic education and basic competence. The gap between the well educated and the masses will widen. If the gap is not narrowed, the manager faces prospects of increasing conflict.

3. Because most advanced economies are not generating adequate surplus value, there will be a shortage of capital to meet growing consumer needs. Any further erosion of the capital base by inflation poses serious danger.

4. As individuals seek multiple and varied career experiences, loyalty to the organization may decline. The time for careful identification, development, and assessment of future leaders will be curtailed.

THE ENVIRONMENT

1. Government intervention in business through regulation and direct intervention will increase. Certain "weak sisters" in an industry may be sustained for reasons determined by government to be in the national interest.

2. Professional associations, representing groups such as lawyers, engineers, and accountants, will make more aggressive demands on managers.

3. There will be a progressive dismantling of centralized decision-making by the organization because power is moving from the center outward to managers of those subunits where the decision impacts most significantly. In Europe the decision-making function of management will be increasingly influenced by growing worker participation.

4. Humanity is moving toward a "communications" society

where the bits of information available to each man, woman, and child on the globe will increase ten- to fifteenfold by 1984. Dealing with the members of this communications society most effectively will be a major challenge to management.

5.   The traditional skepticism toward the managers of the profit-oriented organizations may soften when, in the presence of rising expectations and diminishing resources, societies recognize the importance of the wealth-creating function. However, any perceived inability to "deliver" may generate even greater skepticism toward business. The persistence of ideologies alien to a relatively free market system suggests that critics of business will be ready to exploit every situation where managers are perceived to be ineffectual.

6.   Persistent instabilities in the international monetary system are likely to make the managerial role more difficult.

7.   While organizations like the EEC demonstrate growing awareness of man's interdependence, there is also clear evidence of a spirit of increasing nationalism. Related to (albeit not necessarily dependent on) nationalism are domestic pressures and economic dislocations that engender policies of protectionism and isolationism.

8.   Demographic data reveal declining birthrates. Certainly in the industrialized nations a "graying" population means that fewer workers will be asked to support more nonworkers.

9.   Related to the above is a greater number of unemployables (persons who are alienated, drug-addicted, alcoholic, and the like). Bringing such persons into a constructive role in the work force is a major challenge to management, unions, and government.

10.   Conflicts among diverse cultural and moral systems are intensifying. And despite signs of a growing rejection of organized religions, there are also portents of a more assertive role over business by religious forces. While very clear in the Mideast and in South America, this assertiveness is also visible in Western Europe and in the United States. Managers must therefore deal with articulate and idealistic religious leaders whose concern for persons leads to hostility toward organizations perceived as impersonal.

Today's Realities

What are managers doing today? The following statements highlight the responses of business managers and scholars.

1. Despite widespread cynicism and despite sharp variations among industries and among nations, managers continue to express faith and confidence in their abilities to promote both the good of the organization and the good of society. Nevertheless, when confronted by a hostile environment, managers still behave more in a reactive than a proactive mode.

2. Managers are aware of their need to respond more imaginatively to situations when corporate, social, and personal values conflict. While managers are responding, they acknowledge that much more must be done in this area. At present, two different patterns are developing to meet the needs of managers at the middle level:

- In Europe mid-level managers are beginning to unionize, a trend that may expand elsewhere.

- A second response is managerial job enrichment, achieved by giving managers greater responsibility (see chapter 8).

3. A corollary development is that managers are responding to a basic human need, identified as the individual's right to participate in making decisions and policies that affect his or her destiny, by greater and greater decentralization and equalization of authority.

4. Managers have made the public relations function substantially more sophisticated than it was a decade ago by engaging in a two-way process: communicating *and* listening.

5. Managers, especially at the mid-management level, are also educators. To discharge that teaching function effectively, managers themselves are trained more broadly than more narrowly and view themselves more as generalists than as specialists.

6. Managers are learning how to negotiate — not simply with shareholders and workers, but with other constituencies.

7. Managers realize that the legitimacy of their authority and their function is conferred not simply by law but by the consensual support of relevant constituencies. However, a morale problem has developed for mid-managers because they receive, or at least perceive, mixed signals from the top on matters relating to broad corporate social responsibilities.

8. Because of the complexity of the issues, managers are:

- Moving responsibility for decision-making from the individual to the team;
- Making greater use of part-time advisory bodies to help on special issues;
- Formalizing processes of consultation with workers and making these consultative arrangements distinct from labor-management bargaining.

9. Managers of various kinds of organizations are paying greater attention to career development of employees through such devices as job rotation, special assignments, in-house and external training programs, and the like.

10. In some countries there is greater interorganizational consultation among chief executive officers.

11. Concomitantly, there is more active and widespread participation in the political process by managers at all levels.

12. Many firms (particularly in England and France) are taking steps to prepare employees for different managerial and entrepreneurial careers outside their own organization. Such steps include specialized training, financial help in starting a new business, provision of certain technical skills by consultants drawn from the parent organization, and the like.

13. Multinational corporations are making progress, albeit slowly, in the use of indigenous managerial talent. Complex systems models are being developed to extract what is useful for meeting large-scale problems such as energy, environment, transportation, and related matters.

14. Managers are responding to changes in the composition of corporate boards by arranging for intensive in-depth studies of corporate policies, practices, and problems. Management recognizes that more innovative techniques are required if full effectiveness by board and management is to be achieved.

15. Managers recognize that while business is not simply geared toward "bottom-line" results, the bottom line cannot be ignored. On the manager's ability to produce a reasonable return on investment, in the form of profit or other social benefits, hinges a society's ability to meet legitimate demands: the individual's material needs for a decent life, government's needs for adequate revenue, and the common need for new capital to achieve growth.

Tomorrow's Challenges: Critical Questions and Possible Responses

Because so many challenges confront managers, there is a temptation to write a job description that the Deity itself might find difficult to fill. For, in truth, managers face contrary and contradictory pulls from the organization, from society, and from the aspirations and ambitions of individuals.

What follows is an attempt to provide a realistic definition of management, taking into account three factors: (1) *role and function*, (2) *morale and satisfaction*, and (3) *authority, legitimacy, and governance*. The following subsections spell out more concretely what the three items involve.

ROLE AND FUNCTION

1. To demonstrate their competencies, managers should organize, direct, and lead the enterprise toward the goal of long-term net return on the resources the enterprise employs. By net return we mean:

- Return a fair dividend or increase in net worth to shareholders;
- Enrich and expand employee satisfaction;
- Optimize consumer satisfaction;
- Increase productivity.

2. Since conflicts will occur at times as managers seek to meet all four objectives, the task becomes one of balancing claims from the different constituencies. Clearly, however, the *effective "use" of individuals* is recognized as the most important of the three factors of production (labor, land, and capital).

3. A special function of management is the continual and effective appraisal of its strengths and weaknesses to the end that the strengths are fully employed and the deficiencies quickly corrected. In particular, managers must capitalize on a firm's history. Retaining satisfied customers over a long-term span requires deep appreciation of the organization's special assets. This sense of history is especially critical when there is rapid turnover at the senior executive level.

MORALE AND SATISFACTION

1. Managerial commitment and morale must be aggressively fostered despite the following obstacles:

- Misperception of the manager's role by others;
- Defensive attitudes by managers toward themselves and toward their important work in and for society;
- Systems that do not reward outstanding work or discipline unsatisfactory performance;
- Passivity toward a generally hostile cultural/political environment.

2. Related to the problem of morale are two special circumstances: (1) a growing alienation among managers at the middle levels, especially in Europe; and (2) concern that managers may be losing zest and enthusiasm for their work. Managers must, therefore, deliberately seek to recapture a sense of personal and professional renewal. Since morale starts with the individual and moves to the organization — not the reverse — managers must give more attention to this dimension.

3. Because employees demand opportunities for self-fulfillment, managers are required to give special attention to problems of morale and motivation. Advances in the social sciences (and particularly in psychology) will be monitored and appropriately applied by managers.

AUTHORITY, LEGITIMACY, AND GOVERNANCE

1. Legitimacy is earned only through continual performance for excellence. As never before, managers are part of a team effort whose performance is judged by (1) economic success and (2) moral integrity. Support from constituencies comes as they judge an organization to be responsible and fair because its managers are committed to a high ethical code.

2. Since legitimacy is defined and determined within particular cultural environments, managers contribute constructively to the shaping of those environments.

3. The heartland (terrain) of management operations will move inexorably from the center of the organization to its periphery as the manager is summoned to serve both as a signal-caller to — and a signal-receiver from — the firm's external environment. The manager will deal with politicians and special-interest groups within his or her own country as well as with politicians and special-interest groups of other nations.

4. A primary obligation for managers is to communicate effectively with their multiple constituencies. This requires:

- Creation of internal systems that, through decentralized decision-making and reliable feedback, define goals that are understood and accepted by all;
- Skill in communicating to different constituencies on multiple issues and on a knowledge base that encourages understanding of other economic systems, other ideologies, and other codes of values;
- Explanation by managers of their special mission and their specific obligations to their own particular claimants.

IMPLICATIONS FOR MANAGEMENT SCHOOLS AND FIRMS

1. While managers will require those traditional attributes of intelligence and integrity, energy and adaptability, courage and competence, they will need to mesh more effectively than ever both *cognitive* and *affective* skills. This suggests two things:

- Business faculties must ask themselves how, if at all, affective skills are taught and where they are best acquired.
- So far as cognitive skills are concerned, if we are not talking about philosopher-kings, we are surely talking about philosopher-barons — people well trained and well motivated, hard-nosed yet compassionate, equally adept with tongue and ear.

2. Recognizing that the definition of our future manager may be so all-encompassing and so ambitious that it is unattainable for most people, the organization must construct job definitions that permit optimal contributions from each member of the management team so that the final result is equal to (or better than) the one provided by the "ideal" manager.

3. Adequate preparation for a career in management requires educational centers to produce graduates who:

- Possess skills that justify their initial employment;
- Recognize their needs for continual learning;
- Seek a form of knowledge in the learning experiences that is holistically oriented.

4. More innovations in higher education and more effective articulation among the units of the teaching community will be required so that the delivery systems will respond to the pre-job and post-job experiences of individuals. There are, at a minimum, four identifiable methods to provide management education:

- Professional schools — law, medicine, accounting, education, and the like;
- Schools or centers that concentrate exclusively on providing management training;
- In-house programs such as are found today among several major corporations;
- On-the-job *(in situ)* training.

While variations of the above already exist, coordination among these diverse delivery systems is woefully inadequate; correcting the inadequacy constitutes a major challenge.

5. Among other likely changes are the following:

- Job recruitment and selection, now done mainly on the basis of grades, school, and short interviews, will be expanded to include systematic appraisal of the individual's communication skills, interpersonal capabilities, and sense of ethics.
- The organization's "culture" must be radically redefined so that all employees realize that learning for a future job is as important as performance on the present job.
- Incentive systems must be overhauled so that the values of the new social cultures are reinforced.
- New research will be needed for the early identification of managerial abilities so that career paths can be planned more systematically.

6. Implications for educators are no less significant than they are for leaders of organizations. Among things to be considered by teachers are the following:

- The adequacy of the present admissions tests by business

schools, which assess cognitive skills but do not measure the *affective* skill of students;

- The need to include in the basic curriculum (1) advanced training in bargaining theory and in negotiating skills, (2) sophisticated understanding of ethics and morality, and (3) greater attention to other cultures, including the *use* of foreign languages;
- Structured interactions with other faculties and other disciplines and incentives to business faculty to engage in such interactions;
- Research into new areas that reflect the holistic approach. For example, rarely have social scientists analyzed community life in terms employed by the utilitarians (i.e., stress on the interplay of individual choices) or in terms of hermeneutics (i.e., the nature of social activity depends on the chief actors' understanding of it).

7. Because the connections between business and other organizations and between public and private sectors are deepening, opportunities for education and experience in different types of activities should be systematically offered by both universities and organizations.

8. Because of expanding professionalization, the managers of the future will need to be taught the values and "styles" of other professionals to the end that their organizations make the most effective use of these ancillary, but important, resources.

Some Additional Implications

SMALL BUSINESS

Because the contemporary business system is so much influenced by large corporations and particularly by the transnationals, a conclusion might be drawn that small business might slip into insignificance and that preparation of managers for small firms represents a diversion from the main objectives of management education. On the contrary, it is likely that small business will not only persist but will grow in importance because it is essential to a dynamic economy. Therefore, management education for this sector in all economies has to receive careful attention.

WOMEN IN THE WORK FORCE

A new and exciting explosion has occurred in the work force as vastly more women — because of desire or need — have moved to careers outside the home. Talented and resourceful, these women demand equal job opportunity, equal pay for equal work, equal opportunity for advancement. Most visible in the industrialized countries today, this phenomenon will undoubtedly spread throughout the world.

No one can predict with absolute certainty what women will bring to management careers, and no one is certain what influence the surge of women into the marketplace will have on family life, on schools, on churches, and on organizations. Certainly, the women show little or no inclination to ask organizations to make adjustments to their special talents or their special needs. Encouraging the women to use their best talent and backing up the rhetoric with innovative policies may turn out to be one of the most important challenges to Western leaders during the coming decade.

UNEMPLOYMENT — UNDEREMPLOYMENT

While the effective use of human beings constitutes the manager's most important challenge, there is a need to restate the challenge in broader terms. Reflecting a growing sentiment, the distinguished biologist, Rene Dubos, once said: "I regard unemployment as the most serious problem of modern society, even more destructive — paradoxical as it may sound — than nuclear warfare, shortages of resources, and environmental degradation." Dubos concluded that "the opportunity to perform a useful role in the social structure is an essential condition of mental health — one of the inalienable human rights" (*American Scholar* [Autumn 1979], pp. 440, 446).

While less harsh in its consequences, underemployment also poses a serious challenge. As more people become more educated, the need to draw maximum performance from each person will be intensified, and managerial skills will be tested — and measured — by responses to this particular problem.

THE THIRD WORLD

As Ignacy Sachs pointed out earlier in this volume, the developing countries represent an awakening giant. If humanely and imagi-

natively handled by managers and public leaders of the industrialized countries, the giant can lend powerful shoulders to forward
economic and political growth on a world scale. If the giant's values
are contemptuously treated — or underrated — the global arena
will become a test of naked power where, in the long run, no true
victor will emerge. Often Third World leaders suggest (as do sup-
porters, for example, of liberation theology in South America) that
a new international morality, based on redistribution of wealth to
developing countries, is required. If the proposed morality seems
a bit one-sided to Westerners, it should be recalled that the "haves"
face only two choices in dealing with the Third World: to accept
the proposed redistributionistic ethic or to work with developing
countries in a partnership that increases goods and services and
shares such increases equitably.

THE MARKET SYSTEM

Concern for the Third World has given rise to a very delicate and
sensitive topic — namely, the hostility of many in the developing
nations toward the market system and the fact that much of this
hostility, while emanating from the Third World, actually origi-
nates in the West itself.

The practical conclusion is this: As "Western" managers must
understand the values espoused by others, including collectivism,
so must others understand the market's philosophical premises and
its structural contours. When economic interdependence increases,
competition on an international scale will likely intensify; this, in
turn, will be characterized by competition among state-owned corporations of Eastern Europe, state-supported corporations of Japan,
and the more nearly autonomous firms located in Western Europe
and North America working closely with their respective national
governments.

ENTREPRENEURSHIP

Because the entrepreneur has provided so much of the vitality to
the economics of both Europe and North America, it is obvious
that neglect of the entrepreneurial role in an organization would
entail unfortunate consequences. This neglect is possible because
many are coming to believe, with the late Arnold Toynbee, that

large corporations clearly dominate the contemporary scene; therefore, the structural reality is pervasive bureaucracy. Big bureaucrats are served by petty bureaucrats. Both the organization and the professional schools have serious obligations to analyze the nature of the entrepreneurial function because future managers, in all forms of organizations, will need those entrepreneurial skills that create markets. If there are no customers, no clients, no patients, the organization withers.

GEOGRAPHIC AND CULTURAL DIFFERENCES

While managers will increasingly possess a certain common body of knowledge and skill, it is recognized that such knowledge and such skill will be put to work in environments having marked differences. Appreciating those differences — and respecting them — will be a prerequisite for effective management in the future.

Retaining Perspective

As one ranges over the array of conclusions drawn by the various contributors to this volume, it becomes increasingly clear that the manager of the future is being defined in large terms — and with bold strokes. To fulfill the role effectively, the manager must know how to motivate people, organize resources, create markets, deal with governments, respond to special interests, recruit talent, understand different cultures, and discern major trends.

The meetings between Europeans and Americans, on which this volume is based, were the first of their kind and therefore endowed with a historic quality. But there may be more to their importance than is even now perceived, because discussion may lead to profound reassessments of the three conceptual pillars on which the contemporary liberal society is built:

- A theory of self;
- A theory of society;
- A theory of knowledge.

A comment on each is appropriate.

THEORY OF SELF

Modern man has been profoundly influenced by Adam Smith's definition of the person as one primarily concerned with enlightened self-interest. Without denying the importance of this view, one might add that the concept of the self must accommodate itself to what Martin Buber called the "I-Thou" equation. More concretely, fulfillment of the self *necessitates* involved fulfillment by others; "anything done to diminish another diminishes me." A body of contemporary psychology and what is sometimes called "processive" theology both affirm that self-enrichment comes only as others are enriched.

Is this new perception simply a clever way to rationalize or refurbish the old "human relations" approach of past management education? I think not. What was objectionable in the early approaches were hints of manipulation of human beings and use of incentives to induce human beings to do things "my way." The subtleties of the contemporary approach lie in the emphasis on doing things "our" way through goals mutually determined, methods mutually acceptable, and for results that are mutually rewarding.

THEORY OF SOCIETY

Certain theories of society, which gained ascendancy in the last three or four centuries, were postulated on a view of society built on adversarial relations: Businessmen relied on competition; politicians depended on party rivalry; lawyers sought justice through adversarial techniques; even love was described as "war between the sexes."

Implicit in the old tradition was emphasis more on role than on individuality or personhood. Suggestions are now being made that while an adversarial society has provided substantial gains, it lacks elements that give cohesion to life. The word *holistic*, which surfaces frequently in this volume, is simply a recognition that anomie seems to be a fact of contemporary life for many people and that the hunger for community is powerful and widespread.

What social instrument can provide that sense of community? In the past it was the family and the church. For the future it may be the state, because governments are called upon to serve as the primary vehicle to promote social justice.

No one can see with certainty what contours the new state will take. But the fact that so much mention has been made of state involvement in business affairs would suggest, at a very minimum, that steps toward viewing the state as the primary instrument of justice have already been taken.

The critical questions for the future are these:

- What can the state do most effectively that no other organization can do?
- What can the corporation do that no other organization can do?
- What can the partnership or joint venture do more effectively than any other organization can do?
- What is the special role for voluntary nonprofit organizations?

The list could, of course, be extended.

THEORY OF KNOWLEDGE

It is a gross oversimplification to suggest that one man has defined the nature of the "modern mind" — which is empirical, quantitative, rationalistic. If one dared to suggest a candidate, certainly high on the list would be Rene Descartes. What is interesting about the Cartesian revolution was the fact that Descartes' dualism encouraged modern man to go about the world's work. If there were two realities — spiritual and material — then, said Descartes, matters of the spirit could not be measured, quantified, or empirically demonstrated. Careful not to deny the possibility of such a reality, Descartes nevertheless encouraged scholars to concentrate on the here-and-now. From the Cartesian revolution flowed swift currents to carry human understanding of the nature of the universe and of the self.

There is now a concern that a redress is in order and that matters not so readily measured or quantified are important: ambition, self-respect, creativity, community, compassion, sacrifice. How the synthesis will be achieved is indeed very unclear. Some feel that affective learning cannot be pursued in a classroom setting because it comes only through experience; others deny this premise. The debate will intensify and will be conditioned by the advances made in understanding the human personality.

Yet the very understanding may generate a new irony, because personhood is so often ambiguous. The capacity to live within a community, to accept painful compromise without compromising the organization's integrity, and the ability to lead self-affirming persons toward common goals — all these qualities in the future manager depend on advancing the frontiers of understanding.

In moments of great transition there has been present in the Western tradition a rather interesting phenomenon — a revival of liberal learning. Since liberal learning addresses itself to analysis of fundamental human values (such as justice and liberty, equality and community), such revivals have always brought renewed interest in ancient sources: Greek writings and the Bible.

While it is difficult to predict what direction liberal learning will take, certainly it is true that management itself will depend on the resources flowing in the liberal tradition. As the effort moves slowly, one might legitimately ask the question: Are we on the margins of a new Enlightenment? If the answer is yes — as many believe it is — then the endeavor that this volume represents is a significant and historic intellectual enterprise.

CHAPTER 12

Management and Holistic, Lifetime Learning

BORIS YAVITZ

One carries away from an international meeting of managers and management educators a mental notebook in which are written some of the key conclusions or special insights one has found particularly useful. With time the contents of that notebook will be expanded and sharpened. While incomplete, the central messages of the notebook seem, even now, clear enough.

Demand

The pattern of demands any society makes of its managers is largely shaped by such forces as the following:

- Mass communication explosion;
- Spreading egalitarianism;
- Rising sense of entitlements;
- Increased power by a growing number of constituencies through the control of scarce resources.

These forces generate *expectations* (by societies, by interest groups within societies, and by individuals) that, I suggest, are qualitatively different from our past experience. They represent discontinuities from historical trends, in terms of:

- How *much* is expected;
- How *fast* it must be delivered;
- To how *many* it must be delivered;
- How *divergent* in nature are the expectations.

These expectations are inevitably translated into a set of conflicting, often ambiguous, but always insistent, *demands* — demands that each society makes of its institutions and organizations and, by extension, of its leaders and managers.

Consider now the nature of the political responses to perceived demands, at least in reasonably democratic societies:

- Candidates for political office fan the flames of expectations with promises.
- Elected officials try to "deliver" on promises in very short-run and highly tangible terms. Members of the U.S. Congress, for example, with two-year terms of office, are in effect continually acting as both candidates and office-holders.
- Attempting to satisfy demands in this political fashion leads to considerable waste, erosion of resources, and disjointed efforts. More importantly, government lays out a zig-zag, inconsistent course by providing organizations with a series of shifting, shadowy, moving targets. This accounts for the frustrating sense of "hunting" (in the engineering sense), which seems to permeate many organizational objectives. We move in one direction, over-

shoot it, and come back — only to find that the target has moved again. The endless chase continues.

Supply

The supply side of the equation concerns itself with the resources and talents that must be assembled in order to satisfy social expectations and demands. It seems apparent that the marshaling and directing of these resources are becoming increasingly more difficult and complex tasks.

Capital, materials, energy, information, knowledge, human resources, and skills must be deployed to produce any output. Each of them is becoming more difficult to obtain and more complicated to integrate into a balanced whole. Some are in short supply; others are rising in price. More importantly, they can no longer be bought for money alone. They need to be *bargained* for in a complex bundle of exchanges. We often find ourselves paying with technology transfer for raw materials, with satisfaction for human labor, and with political concessions for capital.

A much subtler set of negotiations and imaginative barters will be needed to put together the productive capacity of the enterprise than the simple purchase of required resources.

Environment

What of the manager's role in the emerging environment? All our discussion indicates that tomorrow's manager must achieve much more than the already difficult task of producing goods and services of appropriate quality and at optimal efficiency. Beyond that, he or she must constantly strive for that delicate balance between the demands of all constituencies or stockholders. The manager simply cannot afford to maximize the interest of any single constituency at the cost of others. The manager's role calls for optimizing the total mix — and always in the long-range terms and within accepted norms of fairness and equity.

Reviewing my own arguments, I seem to be describing a world in which the manager is the guardian of the common good and the far-sighted shaper of strategic progress. The politician, on the other hand, is perceived as the expedient "hit-and-run artist" and the

pawn of parochial pressure groups. A topsy-turvy world: The manager as statesman — the politician as spoiler?

This is a distinct role reversal from the usual view of the world
in the Western liberal tradition. Conventional wisdom has always
warned of the businessman's parochial, short-term, profit-only orientation — which had to be tempered by government as the guardian of all the people in the long-run interest of national goals.

I need to note here that I am not preaching a Second Coming
of the "technocrats" as the true saviors of society, *à la* Thorstein
Veblen. Veblen's technocrats were inherently wise, just, and competent, and thus could themselves judge what was "right" for society. The managers I foresee arrive at what is "right" through
extensive communication, consultation, and bargaining with the
varied stakeholders they represent. The result is certainly not a
"technocracy." It could, perhaps, be aptly labeled "managerial democracy" — an era beyond the so-called industrial, postindustrial
democracies.

The role of the manager envisaged here represents quite a challenge — particularly when it must be performed within the conventional, hierarchical status that sets government as the "franchisor"
and business as the "franchisee." We are describing, in reality, another quality and talent for the manager: "upward leadership." The
intriguing question is this: how to get one's superior to behave in
a responsible way when one is the acknowledged subordinate. It
should be emphasized that we are describing managers at *all levels*
of the organization, not simply the chief executive. This implies
an organization that is not pictured as a sharp-edged pyramid, but
one that resembles a free-form organism with a highly permeable
skin or membrane. It is, therefore, no longer valid to view the operation manager as "the one in the middle" — pressured by profit
and social demands from the top and by the demands of workers
from the bottom. Rather, managers at all levels will be interacting
(through the permeable skin) with many constituencies, both
within and without the organization. Communications — two-way
communications — are the essential ingredients that permit the
manager to function within this porous membrane.

Education

Implications to education are many and have been neatly summarized in the foregoing chapters. Let me simply note some evolv-
ing trends in the education of managers for the future:

- Greater emphasis on the ability to communicate both ways (listen, sense, understand external needs as well as explain, articulate, and persuade).
- Improved negotiating, bargaining, and arbitrating skills: consensus-forming, political balancing, finding effective solutions to multiconstituency problems. These skills need to be applied externally as well as within the organization.
- A more holistic and strategic approach in dealing with organizational problems. This implies placing functional plans in the context of the organizational whole, maintaining an international rather than a local perspective, and providing a multistakeholder rather than a single-interest advocacy. All these tasks must be viewed in strategic, longer-run perspectives rather than as a series of discrete tactical maneuvers.
- An appreciation of the need for both cognitive and noncognitive (or affective) learning. Much needs to be done to determine what can be taught, what can only be learned, and the most effective ways for achieving both.
- Finally, the education of the manager must be increasingly viewed as a continuous, integrated process. The division of education into graduate versus undergraduate, pre- versus postexperience, university versus corporation, and classroom versus on-the-job compartments is artificial. It may be the way we currently do things. It is not the way an individual actually learns over time and career spans. The implication of this is clear: closer coordination between universities, institutes, executive programs, on-the-job training, postexperience seminars, and in-house corporate education. The British "teaching corporation" provides an interesting experiment in this direction.

There are important corollaries for both education and business. Universities must instill a thirst for learning and motivate the individual to "learn how to learn" over an entire lifetime. Corporations must create a climate that encourages and rewards continual learning.

Conclusion

If our projections of the manager's world are even partially valid, then managers can look forward to living in most interesting times. It is said that one of the cruelest curses in Chinese says: "May you live in *interesting* times." Perhaps so. But "interesting times" are also the driving force of challenge, excitement, creativity, and accomplishment!

All I can tell you is this: if I were twenty years old in the early 1980s, perceived the world ahead of me along the lines we have sketched out here, and could avail myself of the kind of education we are calling for, there would be little ambivalence in my position. If anybody asked me: "What would you like to do when you grow up?" my answer would be quite clear: *"I want to be a manager!"* And the very next day I would send in my application to the Columbia Business School!

PART III

Management Education and Development for the XXI Century

CHAPTER 13

Challenges to Educational Institutions

JACQUES CHABAN-DELMAS

What kinds of business leaders and public officials do we need and will we need to direct our companies and organizations — at every level — and lead them toward efficient and harmonious human and economic development? What responsibilities should fall to the management schools for this purpose? What methods of work and plans of action must schools and centers adopt in order to make progress?

If these questions are paramount, we must stress their decisive character and moral aims. Americans as well as Europeans share the desire to promote the vital necessity of enterprises that are competitive and therefore efficient, and at the same time to ensure the primacy of man in freedom and dignity.

The context in which these questions are asked, as well as the risks we are likely to encounter, deserve to be clearly stated. We place our discussions in the quite ambitious perspective of the coming thirty years. Even taking into consideration the fortunately growing possibilities offered by continuing education, it is proper, in thinking about the future, to start being vigilant about the pedagogical orientation of management schools.

Thinking about the future has already given rise to many studies and numerous assumptions. The difficult period in which we have been living since the earlier 1970s cannot in any way be considered a crisis period. A crisis is short-lived. The constraints of all kinds, domestic and foreign, that our countries are undergoing will be with us for some time. To analyze them suitably, to appreciate their implications, to face up to them serenely and willingly — such are the prerequisites that should be taken into consideration by those wishing to master their fate and not to submit passively to exogenous factors.

The economy, international relations, and the place of education in our societies offer, in this respect, several themes for reflection. In the long run, the survival of our societies is closely related to the strength of our economies — that is to say, to the strength of our enterprises. Bluntly stated, without business competing in the marketplace, there cannot be any lasting production of wealth, individual or collective. The prosperity, the progress, and the identity of a nation cannot in any way be separated from its ability to compete. Let us prepare and train the work force in our respective countries for this requirement. At the same time, whether we speak of the demands of liberty, dignity, consideration, or equality — common legacy of the countries of Europe and of North America — never has the human dimension assumed such a strong timeliness and intensity as in this last part of the twentieth century. Reconciling the continuing search for competitiveness with the strengthening of man's dignity in his work and in society will constitute a major challenge.

If we observe the relations between nations, we see that the level of international exchange is often a sign of prosperity. The example of the members of the European Economic Community illustrates this point. For the member countries, the creation and development of the community has led to an exceptional growth of commercial, industrial, and technical exchanges and the exchange of persons. Better training of our future managers in international relations is essential. Whether European or American, managers should be aware of responsibilities toward the developing countries, which are often faced with critical problems in organizing their businesses and their governments. The mere acknowledgment of the community of interests that binds us to the Third World, the determination to organize a world order in quest of peace, the necessary correction of the most flagrant injustices and inequalities — all of these compel us to enhance those activities and responsibilities that may contribute to strengthening the potential of the developing countries. Here is another responsibility, and at the same time a second challenge.

Lastly, we should mention the place of educational institutions and the role they are to play as we look ahead to the future. In several of our countries, we have diagnosed our educational systems as being insufficiently adapted to our needs. The degree and the causes of this deficiency differ from one country to the other. All of us are conscious of the necessity of reevaluating our schools and our universities, and the training of young people as well as adults. Managerial training is a part of our national educational systems, several of which are in need of reform in order to build a new society well adapted to the technological needs, as well as to the human and spiritual needs, of the new universe now coming into being.

Facing these challenges, European and American officials responsible for the training of managers have at their disposal quite a few assets. Hence, we may rightfully ask of them a real contribution to the efficiency and well-being of our industrial and social development.

Managers and management educators have four assets at their disposal, and the fourth may become the decisive one.

First asset: They are able to compare their experiences and reflections with those of others, in their own countries as well as internationally. By its very definition, isn't it a characteristic of true management to communicate, to exchange, to learn from others? In this context we should pay tribute to the role played by the Ford Foundation in promoting management training in universities, first in the United States and then in many European countries. This is also the purpose of the American Assembly of Collegiate Schools of Business, headed by Dean Vernon Zimmerman. In Europe, the European Foundation of Management Development, a pragmatic and nondirective body, which promotes meetings and intellectual interchanges, should be congratulated on the quality of its work. Its president, Arnoud Caron, can be proud of directing the European Foundation with such ease, a quality that distinguishes truly talented and devoted men, and of course with so much efficiency. Supported by national foundations, different in each country but motivated by the desire to bring together universities and corporations as well as the public and private sectors, the European Foundation for Management Development should play a growing role in the coming years.

Second asset: Management training involves a well-tested ability to link a mastery of technical tools with a sound organizational ability and the preeminence of human values in the workplace. In the last twenty years the tools of management and production have multiplied and have become increasingly sophisticated. Just think of the evolution of financial and accounting techniques, of computer sciences, or of telecommunications. Management also means a mastery of tools and techniques by man, and not the opposite. Thus, management training must be able to master the techniques in order to firmly establish man's role. This ability is a question of ethics. That is why I attach so much importance to it.

Third asset: Management training involves a continuing exchange between teachers and practitioners of business. An analogy with medicine is pertinent. Is it possible to get good medical teaching divorced from the reality of the care of patients and hospitals? It is not by chance that medical teaching and hospitals are placed side by side. Good management teaching implies continuing contributions from business and experience, but it also needs a theoretical underpinning. That is why our American friends were the first to demonstrate in the past that universities can and must play a major role in management training. The American experience, well known in France, has prompted the useful transfer of management training to French universities. We should congratulate ourselves on this point. Whether or not these management training centers are connected with universities, they will be able to adjust to changes insofar as they strengthen their relations with business and improve the quality of their faculty.

Fourth asset: As mentioned earlier, this asset could be the decisive one. Management is not the panacea only for industrial or commercial companies. Armies, churches, universities, government, trade unions, and social and nonprofit organizations need the right kind of management. Their leaders must devote their energies to achieving objectives appropriate to these types of organizations.

A nation is sound and well prepared for the future if the leaders of these public and private organizations can, while achieving their own aims, carry on a useful dialogue, speak a common language. In the vision of the future that you and I share, management and management training are the tools of liaison and dialogue, of change and social progress. It is up to each one of us to know how to take advantage of the totality of the existing or potential assets of our management training centers.

In conclusion, I would like to stress three main points. Depending on temperament and cultural background, one can find in them goals to promote, precautions to take, or risks to avoid.

The first point is *elitism*. The *dirigeants*, as they say in French — the *managers*, as they are called in English — are the subject of our attention. This word applies to the highest executives in firms and organizations. One of our aims is to attempt to promote the most appropriate training programs for them. But do not forget, as the English terminology indicates, that management involves everyone. We can apply to management the observation made by Michel Crozier on entrepreneurship: It "has to be understood not as an attitude linked with any particular social group but as a widespread common value, society's equivalent of the salt of the earth; and everything must be done to make this value accessible to the largest number of people possible."

The assumption of responsibility, entrepreneurship, and management will have to be increasingly the concern of a greater number of individuals. Should we view this as a cultural and political necessity as well as a moral imperative?

The second point is *openness*. Teachers quite rightly want to reinforce and make known their seriousness of purpose and professionalism. Who would not encourage such efforts? But we must undoubtedly ensure that the professionalism of educators and teachers remains fully open to the changing nature of society, not only in its cultural and social dimensions but also in its scientific and technological dimensions.

There may be deviations or excesses of all kinds, and we must ensure that they do not impair or call into question the quality of management training. What we are talking about, of course, is a state of mind. It is — and the work of the European Foundation shows it clearly — a question of the organization of the training centers and of the choice, background, and diversity of the faculty. It is obvious that the quality and suitability of programs in initial and continuing training cannot be considered in isolation from the types of organizational patterns in institutions and in universities.

The final point to be considered is *cultural diversity*. Undoubtedly, this is the most decisive point. Undoubtedly also, the situation varies from country to country, according to its history and national character, as His Holiness John Paul II mentioned recently with such strength and authority. The best data processing systems are, depending on the situation, well or poorly used. They remain the same systems regardless of the country in which they are used. On the other hand, motivating people and exercising responsibility are tasks that cannot be evaluated without reference to their sociocultural or national context. Management schools, especially when their aim is to train people coming from, or destined to work in, different kinds of professional and national environments, must distinguish between what is universal in management and what derives from the particular cultural heritage of countries and cultures. This kind of heritage must be preserved and enriched in carrying forward a historic past that must never be forgotten.

CHAPTER 14

Executives of the Future: An Address

WILLIAM P. TAVOULAREAS

Frankly, I do not know how to be particularly helpful in approaching the subject of the executive of the future. In the years that I have been in the international oil business, my career has been affected far more profoundly by events that no one could have forecast than by the things that an orderly process of planning might have identified beforehand. I would therefore hazard the guess that executives of the future will need to possess the same talents that characterize effective managers today — namely, the *ability* to deal with the unexpected, and the *skills* to assess risks. They will need to make decisions in a way that will protect against the greatest risks and still preserve the opportunity to benefit from those occasional unexpected favorable turns of fate.

Of course, in saying that future executives must be no less agile than their counterparts today, I am in no sense saying that the world of the future will be a world of "business as usual." Indeed, I know that the business environment will be very different from the business environment I have experienced in most of my career.

It is now more than thirty-five years since the end of World War II and the beginning of what was to become an explosive recovery of the industrialized nations of Europe from the ravages of war. As any student of economic history knows, that recovery was dominated by the role of the United States in international affairs. We applied our economic and political concepts to virtually every aspect of economic life overseas, and we received the cooperation of other countries almost without question because of their desire and need for U.S. participation in the economic restoration of the world.

Now the situation is very different. No longer is the United States universally viewed as the senior partner; the Cassandras among us are even telling us that the days of U.S. leadership are over because the United States is becoming too weak. That, of course, is too harsh a view.

By all objective standards, the economy of the United States is huge, and it plays a large role in the economic life of the industrialized world. But there is no question that in *relative* terms the United States is no longer the clearly preeminent factor in international economic affairs that it once was. The major nations of Europe and Japan enjoyed enormous growth as they recovered from their crippled condition after the war, and they are now asserting their right to have an equal voice in the decisions that affect us all.

Adjusting to this new reality has been painful to the United States, and we have not yet completed that adjustment. Congress still finds itself passing bills covering the whole world, without engaging in any prior consultation with other countries, and the president continues to sign bills of that nature with the same sort of indifference to the feelings of others abroad, in spite of his constitutional role to direct foreign policy. Thus, for example, we try to extend overseas the powers of the Securities and Exchange Commission in corporate accounting and the securities laws, the Justice Department and the Federal Trade Commission in areas of antitrust law, the Internal Revenue Service in the area of taxation, and the Federal Corrupt Practices Act in the area of corporate morality. We legislate standards in these areas without any attempt to consider conditions abroad. There was a time when perhaps this sort of thing made sense, when it may have been desirable for the U.S. government to prescribe rules under which American companies would operate both at home and abroad, because American commerce accounted for such a large share of the world's total commerce, and oftentimes such rules did not exist anywhere else in the world.

Now, however, the situation has changed; we are no longer legislating in a vacuum. Thoughtful legislators everywhere have considered the same problems we face and have devised their own solutions to them. Americans have been slow to recognize that the solutions selected by other countries may still be effective, even though they are different. To give one very limited example, there is the matter of taxation of corporations that operate outside the country. Businessmen and economists have long recognized that if a multinational corporation is to be competitive, it must pay the same tax in a local country as the domestic company does, and other tax burdens should not be imposed by the home jurisdiction on that overseas income. If added home country taxes *are* imposed on the foreign income, the effect will be to make the company paying those taxes uncompetitive in the foreign market and will eventually cause it to lose its business and its profits in those markets.

There are basically two ways to prevent this double taxation. Some countries adopt the policy of keeping foreign income outside the tax return so that companies with losses overseas do not get a deduction, but then neither do they pay taxes on the earnings they receive from abroad. This is the theory of tax neutrality.

The United States has adopted a different system. Under this system foreign operations are included in the tax return, but a credit is given against U.S. taxes on the foreign income for the amount of the foreign tax paid. In theory, neither system is superior since the objective in both cases is to avoid the double taxation of earnings. However, in practice, the U.S. Treasury has long since forgotten that the credit system was designed to avoid double taxation, and the bureaucrats are continually seeking ways to deny a credit. Nor is this silliness peculiar to the Executive Department. When the treaty with the United Kingdom was ratified recently, the U.S. Senate insisted on deletion of a provision that would have prevented the individual states in the United States from taxing the earnings of the U.K. corporations operating in the state under the so-called unitary system. Under this system of taxation, the state allocates a portion of the worldwide earnings of the so-called unitary business of a corporation to the state on a formula basis, notwithstanding that the unitary business may be conducted, in part, by a number of different corporate entities around the world. By insisting on a deletion of this provision, the Senate was, in effect, insisting that the United Kingdom must recognize this tax concept devised by certain of the American states. The United Kingdom eventually acceded to the request of the U.S. government, and the provision was deleted.

Nor does the problem end here. Not only does the United States insist that its own system of law is superior to other systems elsewhere, but the regulation of business is also becoming increasingly political. I mentioned earlier the matter of the foreign tax credit. For many years the concept of the credit has been a part of the tax law and has been administered by professionals in the Internal Revenue Service. Now, politicians have argued against giving a credit for taxes paid to certain countries, and they have written complex laws that they hope will make the tax of one country creditable and, at the same time, will deny credit to the tax of another country. This sort of law is not only extremely complex; it also perverts the theoretical basis for our system of taxation.

In a similar way, a provision has been introduced into the revenue code that denies foreign tax credits altogether in the event a company runs afoul of the enormously complex regulations relating to boycotts by certain countries.

Not satisfied with this so-called solution, Congress drew up an additional body of law that is administered by the Commerce Department, imposing its own set of regulations for violations of a different set of antiboycott laws, and any company operating overseas has to make certain that it complies with not one but both of these complex monstrosities — for failure to comply with both will subject the company to horrendous penalties, some of them criminal.

The boycott subject has an element of comic opera inherent in it, because there are a number of different kinds of boycotts practiced in the world, including some administered by the U.S. government itself. There are boycotts that are "desirable," and there are boycotts that are "undesirable." Yet these laws are supposed to be drawn in a general way to deal evenhandedly with all kinds of boycotts.

Clearly, this attitude of legislative arrogance has to change, and in effecting such a change, the greater part of the burden will unfortunately fall on the business executive of the future. There is no one else to inform the Congress and the administration about the realities of the foreign business scene other than the business executives who must operate there. For whether we like it or not, we businessmen and -women will take the blame from our friends overseas for the ineptness of our government in writing rules to regulate the world.

The examples I have given up to this point emphasize the trouble that arises when we try to hang on to the "big brother" role we once occupied, even though our relative power no longer justifies such pretensions. There are still some areas where the size of the American presence is key and where our failure to cooperate effectively is also the cause of much mischief. Perhaps the most important has to do with energy.

The U.S. position as a producer is no longer a dominant factor in world supply, as it was when we exported oil, but our position as a *consumer* has the potential for contributing substantially to disruptions of the world energy market. It can be argued, in fact, that the rapid increase in our gasoline consumption following the adoption of our first auto emission controls was a contributing factor in catapulting the United States into first place as the largest importer of oil in the world — surpassing Japan for the first time.

Similarly, our inability to agree on the environmental rules for the trans-Alaskan pipeline and for offshore leases following the Santa Barbara spill created a long delay in exploiting crude reserves on the North Slope and in the offshore areas and put more demand on imported oil, in competition with the growing needs of other consuming countries.

But U.S. influence in energy is also important in a more subtle way. The clamor that accompanied the development of nuclear power plants in the United States has been suspended in a great many areas. (I would say parenthetically that France is an exception to this suspension — a fact for which all of us may well be grateful in the years to come, when the electricity generated by their nuclear plants will not be competing for limited supplies of liquid hydrocarbons.)

The balance between the available supplies of oil in the world and the demand for those supplies is so delicate that energy is now a major area with potential for conflict among the nations, for our way of life cannot survive without energy. We can conserve, indeed, but when we have become as efficient as we can be, economic growth will dictate that we shall have to continue to use energy to fuel our industry and to heat and light our homes. We badly need to see sound energy policies being pursued aggressively by all the consuming countries, looking to the day when a substantial portion of the demand for oil can be replaced by other sources of energy. When I say "looking to the day," I am not talking about looking so far into the future as to be dreaming. We must have policies grounded on technology we *know*. Of course, we should spend money on research to achieve the breakthroughs we know will come in the future, but we cannot risk the health and economic well-being of the world on technologies that we can only *hope* to discover. In the interim, before the exotic technologies are in hand, we must make use of what we have. And what is that?

First, of course, those countries blessed with coal — including the United States — must utilize coal to generate electric power and to burn in boilers for other purposes, and we must utilize it in a way that is as unobjectionable environmentally as we can reasonably make it. But not all countries have coal.

There is another source of power that can now be utilized to generate electricity — that is, or course, nuclear power. We know how to build nuclear plants, and we have the fuel for them. And because the cost of uranium is such a relatively small part of the cost of electricity, the balance-of-payments impact of nuclear power is very much lower than that of power generated from either oil or coal. Thus, a much larger number of consuming countries can afford to have their own long-term energy sources if nuclear power is used. Of course, there need to be safeguards. We know that *every* energy source is dangerous, but we also know that there are ways to reduce the risks of each of the energy sources. It is my thesis that we must use *all* of the energy sources available to us, and we must adopt the safeguards to make the risks of each of them tolerable. I am also convinced, based upon the knowledge we already have, that this goal is feasible.

It is therefore fitting that we should contemplate the urgent need for the United States to better understand the needs of its friends and allies abroad, to increase its cooperation with them, and to appreciate the benefits that such cooperation can bring to all of us. For if we can just agree in the limited area of energy policy, then the producing countries can look forward to the day when the seemingly endless thirst for energy will not rest totally on their ability to produce greater and greater quantities from the limited reserves they possess. That realization would moderate the pressure for ever-higher prices. It would also mean that the reserves could be called upon for a much longer period to satisfy the most valuable uses for petroleum and to provide revenues to the host countries. On the consuming side, it would provide confidence that the energy needs of the consuming countries can, in fact, be satisfied from known sources for which we can pay — without the risk of conflict and financial chaos.

To fail to agree on energy policy is to bring on confrontation as each of the thirsty consumers jostles with his neighbor to secure the few barrels that remain.

Considering the risks, we have no choice but to try to avoid that confrontation. The message must be understood before it can be passed on, and the executive of the future will be on the firing line of this battle for understanding and cooperation.

CHAPTER 15

The Manager of the Future

BOHDAN HAWRYLYSHYN

To analyze meaningfully so complex a topic as "The Manager of the Future," we have divided the topic into the following four main themes:

- The manager's external functions;
- The manager's internal functions;
- The manager's motivation and morale;
- The kinds of management required by different types of organizations.

This chapter was written by Clarence C. Walton on the basis of an oral presentation by Bohdan Hawrylyshyn.

The Manager's External Functions

Since it is clear that the manager's role in the future depends heavily on the role of the corporation and other organizations in society and that, in turn, the role of such entities depends on the nature of the society in which they operate, it follows that a "steady-state" assumption permits clean-cut analysis to produce rather definitive conclusions. However, the reality is likely to be totally different. No one is quite sure what path societies will take, and questions arise not only about the future of democratic systems in the Western world but also about the possible contours for both socialism and capitalism.

Because the future is seen through a glass darkly, "futurism" is a risky enterprise. For example, the futurists who burgeoned ten years ago have not worn well, and even some of the developments of the past five years were not seen in the various projections made by confident futurists. On the other hand, the onrushing changes constitute a formidable challenge, and a primary purpose of education and of business is to prepare individuals to meet the anticipated — and even the unexpected — as effectively as possible.

Facilitating analysis of the manager's role is a consensus on a fundamental proposition that every societal order is built on different components and that such components rest on certain values. These components and these values combine to produce three needs: (1) a refurbished theory of the person, (2) a more sophisticated theory of the corporation, and (3) a more realistic theory of society. Every social order is literally driven by certain beliefs that encourage certain forms of behavior, and these forms of behavior become typical because they are acceptable. To assure acceptable behavior and to discourage unacceptable behavior, individuals form distinctive kinds of political and economic systems. The following important — and debatable — assumptions may be made:

- The Atlantic world will continue to be characterized by social systems that remain fundamentally unchanged, by highly individualistic and competitive values that will provide the cement for society, and by parliamentary democracies and free enterprise economies.

- The main base of economic power will continue to be private property.

- Government intervention in business will proceed unevenly, but on balance it will probably intensify.

With such assumptions, and with awareness that their acceptance might represent a kind of forbidden extrapolation experience demonstrated to be not very useful, we may move to three major generalizations.

The number and effectiveness of various claimants who stake out their respective demands on the corporation and the state will increase.

From this general proposition come the following ancillary observations:

- Differentiating among the various claimants on the basis of their legitimate demands and not on the basis of their naked power will become a primary responsibility of the manager.
- More utility criteria must be built into decision-making in order to take into account the conflicting claims and different behavioral patterns of various interest groups.
- Relationships between business and government will not lose their adversarial quality, but international developments may force both government and business to cooperate in selected ventures deemed essential to national prosperity.
- Negotiating skills will become extraordinarily important to managerial effectiveness; these negotiating skills will move beyond the normal "one-on-one" relationships (business versus government, unions versus business) to include *simultaneous* negotiations by business with governments, unions, special interest groups, communities, professions, and the like.

Greater diversity than ever will be required for organizational structures, especially for enterprises operating in both national and international arenas.

As restructuring toward shared authority is undertaken, tensions will develop in certain countries because of the following factors:

- Greater government intervention in business affairs and the tendency to hold both directors and executives legally responsible for actions of agents will encourage centralized decision-making. This trend, of course, runs counter to the egalitarian demand for power-sharing.

• A surge of neomercantilism will lead governments to demand that their "essential" industries make certain responses that the market says are ineffective; some demands will increase tensions between public and private officials to such an extent that public confidence in either, or both, will be shaken.

• A possible resurgence of interest in international unionism may induce worker leadership to take a more aggressive stand against management, and managers may thereby be encouraged to keep the reins of their power tightly in control.

The future will bring a sharply rising public demand that every business enterprise be held accountable to society at large and evaluated by criteria that go beyond profit maximization.

From this general proposition flow the following subthemes:

• The concept of corporate social responsibility will be defined in terms that stress voluntary initiatives to meet community needs rather than in terms of simple responses to coercive measures by government or other constituencies.

• A concomitant development will be greater need for more effective analytical skills in defining relationships between business and society.

• Distinctions between creative leadership and routine management will be more sharply defined. Managers of large entities will, in many cases, have to play a leadership role in modes not defined in recent industrial history or understood in traditional theory.

The Manager's Internal Functions

A manager's internal responsibilities will continue to be these three: to mobilize, to develop, and to deploy resources. However, the "style" and the instruments used to fulfill these obligations will change. One need only recall the recent past, when there was much agitation in the business community over the question of "managerial autonomy." At that time fears were expressed that the growing powers of government, unions, professional groups, and special interests were becoming so militant that mangers simply might be unable to manage because of external constraints. The fact that a great deal of stridency has left this debate suggests that business is becoming increasingly aware that rather radical changes in the systems of authority and organizational structures are required. Two basic generalizations may be drawn. Each generalization stimulates, in turn, a cluster of related propositions.

Just as property as the legitimizer of authority evolved into a professional meritocracy rooted in know-how, so, too, will meritocracy yield to industrial democracy as the legitimate basis of authority.

Supplementing the basic proposition are the following:

- Theories of managerial authority (built largely on the writings of scholars like Weber, Fayol, and Taylor) will be replaced by theories that go beyond even the meaning of shared authority expressed in MacGregor's "Theory Y."

- History has demonstrated that a peaceful yielding of authority to other claimants is very difficult because power-holders normally resist any erosion of their jurisdictions. Since managers will share power with others, teaching managers how to make accommodations — while holding others accountable — constitutes a major challenge to educators.

- Although many groups will press claims for more power, there is substantial evidence of a dreary record in the performance of power-holders because those who have acquired power often surrender it to an oligarchy within their own group. Concentric circles of oligarchs may encase managers in very stressful circumstances.

- The further splintering of already splintered groups carries implications of further threats to effective decision-making.

Management style will change from a predominantly hierarchical, authoritarian pattern to a more consultative one in which virtually all actors within the enterprise have opportunities for input.

The following are corollary conclusions to this generalization:

- Recognizing that greater involvement by greater numbers of people may slow parts of the decision-making process, managers will, of necessity, establish their priorities and schedule their work well in advance of desired implementation.
- Since "participative management" means give-and-take, managers will at times be forced to "give" more than they "take" in order to maintain the overall effectiveness of the enterprise.
- In view of the pluralistic nature of the world, there is probably a need to develop more decentralized and flexible organizational structures, which will not be driven by a single sprocket or by a single engine from a single center.

Motivation and Morale of Managers

From the foregoing, it is patent that further complexity will characterize the manager's work in the future. The likelihood of greater frustrations, greater uncertainties, and a declining social status of the manager is real. If this scenario proves accurate, then very important conclusions follow.

The kind of person attracted to management — especially to management in a large corporation — may change because the fundamental nature of the managerial role is changing.

In attracting the most competent people to management, the following considerations are important:

- Management schools should go beyond teaching techniques of administration and should instruct students more deeply in the humanistic dimension of management — that is, they should stress that organizations (and the individuals who compose them) have purposes and needs that must be understood and promoted. Such understanding requires a teleological or goal-seeking dimension.
- The traditional view that managers should not seek to influence the values and philosophies on which society is structured should give way to a realization that managers have as much right as others to mold organizational and social values simply

because they have as vital a stake as others in the health of the societies they serve.

- The past emphasis on utilitarianism (dealing with instrumentalities while leaving others to shape the social order) should diminish. Balancing "direction-giving" and "accommodation" will become important, and success or failure in this balancing act will determine the manager's morale.

Because of greater organizational complexity, it follows that more innovation will be required of managers.

Awareness of this need leads to awareness of a dilemma: Can creativity be taught? While the debate will probably intensify in the future, certain characteristics of creativity can be postulated, and from this base a theoretical structure can be developed. Among the characteristics of creativity are the following:

- Creativity is like intelligence in that it is fairly well distributed across the broad population; thus, teaching it need not be restricted to a predetermined elite.
- While creativity involves rationality, it depends even more heavily on a person's imaginative and affective qualities.
- Creativity is not necessarily restricted to an individual; it can be part of a group process, and lessons can be derived from the way research and development organizations are established and how their people are motivated.
- Some research suggests that people can be trained to become more creative and can learn how to translate creativity into innovation so that an original idea results in some useful product, process, or procedure.

Different Managers for Different Organizations

Recognizing that a society consisting almost exclusively of institutional behemoths could produce strangling kinds of bureaucracy, we must address society's need for management for various kinds of organizations: single proprietorships, partnerships, medium-size businesses, large domestic organizations, transnationals or multinationals, government organizations, nonprofit enterprises, trade unions, and ad hoc organizations that spring up to perform a specific task.

In small businesses, the "boss" knows everyone personally, and adjustments to individual needs can readily be made. Similarly, there are no more than three or four hierarchical levels in the organization of small businesses. On the other hand, because they often have to play the double role of owner and manager, managers of small businesses face certain problems that may be more difficult than those confronting their counterparts in large organizations. Thus, they must be both generalists and specialists. In small enterprises, the boss is often the property owner, and entrepreneur, and the professional manager. Yet each role demands some different qualities and skills. It follows that what small-business managers need to know and the skills they should properly possess are almost boundless; unfortunately, schools of management seem limited in what they can do to teach these skills.

In the case of large businesses, and particularly multinational corporations, managers often have to operate in cultures other than their own and at the same time protect the coherence and cohesion of their own organizations. They must maintain a geocentric kind of organization in a plurocentric kind of world. If the mismatching of organizational structures and organizational needs is to be avoided, managers must be taught how to avoid such pitfalls and how to optimize on a global basis.

Finally, there is the case of government operations and nonprofit enterprises. Like managers of profit-oriented businesses, managers of these organizations must also look for purposeful and effective use of resources to accomplish specified objectives. While the criteria for measuring effectiveness in such organizations are different from those for measuring effectiveness in profit-oriented business firms (e.g., the criteria whereby regulatory effectiveness is measured differ sharply from those used in profit-making organizations), the three types of organizations do interact, and understanding how managerial skills can be transferred from one to the other is important. From these facts a conclusion follows.

The general neglect by schools of management of the needs of small business, government, and nonprofit organizations must end.

To demonstrate their concern, management schools should consider the following:

- Developing special programs in small-business management in which game theory and simulated decision-making are adapted specifically to the needs of managers of small businesses;
- Offering courses on entrepreneurship, including the use of psychology to understand the rewards and pains of risk-taking;
- Pooling in common classes students headed for careers in different organizations so that the learning experiences can be used to probe for an intellectually solid common denominator of skills appropriate to the management of diverse organizations;
- Examining traditional courses in the transfer of technology to determine optimal ways for transferring managerial skills.

In concluding this subject, five major points need consideration.

1. While business management has tended to be very progressive on the technological and economic fronts, it has been conservative toward proposed changes for the sociopolitical field; managers have tended to be defensive and, in some cases, even reactionary. They have projected an image of the business manager as a person whose view of the social universe is limited and whose idea of social and political progress is rooted irrevocably in nineteenth-century liberalism. It is therefore important for managers to convey to the world at large the same kind of creative and innovative patterns they have practiced within their business organizations.

2. In management education networks the emphasis has been utilitarian, and this emphasis has sometimes been carried to an extreme. The result for the business educator has been a field of vision that is too narrow and a reference world that is too constraining. It is important to recognize that the value assumptions that have shaped business philosophy must be monitored. Stability is not one of contemporary society's hallmarks. Even within the last decade there has been a fantastic reversal of trends: from a world of infinite space and infinite resources to a concept of "spaceship earth"; from employing a single country (or two) as a management model for all to the seeming inevitability of a multiplication of models.

3. Related to the foregoing is the rapidity with which change is taking place. Less than a decade ago, the United States provided the model for both the manager and for management education. The reasons for the American preeminence were clear: The United States was a highly productive country; it had helped Europe to upgrade its performances; its postwar economic ascendancy seemed assured. All these characteristics have changed. A number of avant-garde practices are taking place in management on different national fronts. It is perhaps apposite to recall that a Harvard University sociologist — and not a Harvard Business School professor — cited Japan as the prime example of both economic progress and management sophistication. What Japan has demonstrated so dramatically other countries are beginning to try more modestly. Whether the future brings a multiplicity of models, a relevant single model, or the end of all models is unclear. Adaptability and flexibility, however, are obvious needs of transnational organizations.

4. The high-performing countries of the future will be those that learn how to move beyond the adversarial roles between business and government or between business and labor to a more cooperative model. These countries, having learned how to harmonize their objectives, will increasingly insist that the tools for such harmony be accepted by the participating institutional partners. It will indeed require a high form of managerial art to cooperate when cooperation also happens to spur competition.

5. The antenna systems of management education must be broadened to include those educational and management systems existing in other parts of the world. The population of the North Atlantic countries is, after all, less than 10 percent of the world population; its technological and economic leadership must now be matched by a form of managerial leadership that extracts the best elements of diverse cultures. To seek to maintain the North Atlantic as the exclusive reference point is to seek the impossible.

CHAPTER 16

Challenging Issues for Management Education and Development

MAX B. E. CLARKSON

It may be noted that drawing a profile of the future manager is a difficult assignment. That difficulty is equaled, if not surpassed, by efforts to take a profile as a "given" and move forward to determine with some precision what major challenges confront educators as they seek to match need to resources.

The conclusions reached in this chapter are drawn from analyses of problems relating to the following:

This chapter was written by Clarence C. Walton on the basis of an oral presentation by Max B. E. Clarkson.

- Education for specialists and/or generalists;
- Management research and its dissemination;
- Assessment and development of noncognitive learning and its implications for educators;
- International and political dimensions of management education and development.

Specialist or Generalist?

This is a world of explosions — social, political, and economic. No less significant is the fact that even in cultures with relative stability, another propulsive force — the knowledge explosion — is working to produce dramatic consequences. This dynamic aspect of every advanced civilization is producing wide varieties of new professions and subprofessions — each with its own claims to a special competence and each with its own demands for a special autonomy. In such a setting it is logical that students would begin to carefully survey the occupational terrain to determine what specialty is most attractive. In the process, society's need for generalists may take a secondary role.

Resurrected for reanalysis is the historic debate over the primary purpose of education. In the late nineteenth century John Henry Newman's classic answer that liberal education aims to produce men and women of wide learning and deep culture argued for the generalist position. On the Continent different directions were taken. At the University of Berlin, for example, specialization was pursued. The debate is never-ending, and so much has already been said and written about it that further observations have a déjà vu quality. It may therefore appear presumptuous to continue the dialogue, but the very nature of our mission forces a continuing reassessment. Graduates of management schools often run enterprises larger than those of many nations; they operate under a finely spun web of laws and customs; they sustain the tax bases of their countries; they affect the financial future of millions; they deal with exotic raw materials and diverse services. It is not too much to say that managers partake of the quality of "renaissance men." But they begin their careers more modestly in assignments requiring a particular competence. These considerations lead to some important conclusions.

To develop a cohesion of purpose, management schools must provide an education that combines both specialist and generalist strands.

This dual objective creates the following problems:

- Because of the need for entry-level skills, management schools must continue to teach the functional areas of business in order to provide reasonable competency in at least one such field for all their graduates. In addition, the problem of providing a balanced academic diet of specialized knowledge and general management education must be addressed.

- To achieve effectiveness in management education, business faculties often seek cooperation with other faculties, particularly those in the humanities and sciences. Unfortunately, such faculties themselves have shown a tendency toward specialization, and faculty incentives and rewards are developed to foster this bent. Historians have carved their discipline into fragments; philosophers have preferred linguistic analysis to metaphysics or ethics. To secure the best results from cooperative effort requires that the business faculty subtly press their colleagues in liberal arts for acceptable definitions of their goals and for establishment of delivery systems to assure implementation of stated goals.

Management Research and Its Dissemination

To preclude repetitious dialogue on the long-enduring debate over the relative importance of "pure" and "applied" research, let it be said that a dichotomy is intolerable. Every faculty must give attention to both kinds of research. Pure research is a prerequisite because sophisticated theoretical formulations must characterize higher education and because such research often produces unintended practical consequences. Applied research is necessary because management is always action-oriented and recognizes that it is evaluated on the basis of performance.

Three basic points can be established.

While great advances in understanding the decision-making

processes have been made, an even more theoretical and practical understanding of their dynamics is required.

This need arises from the following factors:

- The changing sociopolitical and economic forces that managers confront require an expansion of the parameters of their understanding of decision-making skills. More organization people will be involved; more outside claimants will simultaneously press their demands on business organizations; an overload of data may actually hamper the decision-maker; quantitative decision-making skills must be balanced by qualitative decision-making skills.
- In addition, more experimentation must be done in teaching decision-making and implementation; such experimentation should include the "mixing" of students who represent various organizations with conflicting demands.

Because management is the central resource of developed countries, it follows that their governments should pay considerably more attention to funding research in management on a systematic and nationwide basis.

While resource scarcities must be considered, the following points are also important:

- Declining rates of productivity in some advanced industrialized nations of the world, often attributed to a decline in the work ethic or in capital investment, may be due to ineffective management. When the administrative resource fails, other resources are grossly underutilized. It therefore follows that research in these areas is required.
- Some countries (e.g., Canada) are making progress in developing coordinated plans to foster research. These efforts should be followed carefully by the leaders of other countries and emulated when appropriate.

It is vitally important to establish exchange information systems that permit a flow of information not only on the results of research efforts but also on the results of experiments with new courses and new teaching techniques.

If an international exchange system is established, faculties can benefit from regular interchange with faculties in other parts of the world. In establishing such a system, the following points might be considered:

- Since such a system requires, at a minimum, certain administrative apparatus and facilities, thought should be given to the possibilities of inviting governments to cooperate in providing the necessary resources.

- Professors and graduate students might be released by their institutions for internships in the exchange program because both the institutions and the individuals would benefit.

Noncognitive Learning: Implications for Education

The learning process must be seen in a holistic and integrated way. The early stages of management education, discipline-oriented in order to provide graduates with functional competencies, operate on a simple premise: Competence gives confidence, and confidence gives authority. This competence, in turn, derives largely from a form of cognitive knowledge that can be tested and applied.

However, there is another kind of knowledge, which may be drawn overwhelmingly from experience, that can be neither readily tested nor readily applied. Nevertheless, its essentiality is without question. This form of knowledge may be described as "noncognitive" to distinguish it from those forms of empirical knowledge acquisition that are typically seen in schools of management. The cognitive access to knowledge seems to reach, at a certain stage of the manager's life, a kind of plateau, whereas noncognitive knowledge may offer limitless possibilities.

From this basis we may develop three major propositions.

The "learning" universe must move beyond the present parameter defined by almost exclusive emphasis on cognitive knowledge to include the noncognitive as well. How and where the latter will be learned — and/or taught — requires greater attention from executives and from educators.

The learning universe will expand. Its meaning was suggested by a participant in one of the working groups at the Paris Conference: "We are all sons of Descartes — schooled to accept only analytical reason and empirically tested results as valid knowledge. But Descartes is more like a lonely Adam in a garden of intellect — desperately in need of a helpmate." The learning universe must include both *analytical* and *affective* learning. Noncognitive attributes (such as leadership and administrative skills, oral and written communication skills, attitudes and values, creativity and innovation, ambitions and energies) must be analyzed.

The "unitary" view of learning — understood as learning that occurs in one place, at one time, with one faculty using one curriculum, and concerned primarily with one age group — is obsolete.

This proposition rests on several facts and perceptions, which are illustrated by the following observations:

- Job requirements and/or changing career objectives will lead individuals to follow a learning path that will probably take them from (1) an early stage (acquiring entry-level technical knowledge), (2) through graduate education (broadening that knowledge base), (3) into the working world where experience becomes an added critical factor. Two rather different models for managerial advancement (the British pattern of advancing managers who have progressed within a *single* specialty to the top role, and the American pattern of transferring persons through marketing, finance, production, etc.) will be tested and modified.

- The learning imperative (emphasis on "learning to learn" through life-long learning) will become widely accepted. Schools, recognizing that the incipient manager is only starting a life-long trajectory of learning, may feel less compelled to provide the kind of comprehensive curricula characteristic of earlier times. As a consequence, university-corporation ties will tighten as the business enterprise accepts its obligation to encourage learning.

Institutional leaders will be challenged to develop an even closer partnership between educator and manager.

From this proposition we may derive the following:

- Multicareer patterning must be accompanied by multicareer training.
- No single, self-contained faculty, teaching a single, prescribed academic program, will be positioned to make a satisfactory response.

International and Political Dimensions of Management Education and Development

So evident are the changes coming on the domestic scenes of the various industrialized countries, and so clear are the international pressures on all countries, that to comment extensively on each risks repeating what has been said at many forums on higher education. However, certain of these changes have such direct bearing on management education that two propositions need restatement.

As noted earlier, international competition, extension of the regulatory impact, and changing societal expectations are forcing managers to give more attention to "environment-scanning" programs on issues once deemed unessential to the bottom line.

The following points give added emphasis to this conclusion and have relevance for managers and educators:

- Evidence that perceptive executives have already reached this conclusion and are acting upon it continues to mount. Managers in Western Europe have possibly experienced more business-society exchanges than their counterparts in the United States, but even in that country a historic break came a decade ago when the presiding officers of DuPont, General Electric, General Motors, and AT&T led in establishing the Business Roundtable. This organization is committed to speaking out on issues of public policy. Before "speaking out," it is essential to "think through" — and in this latter step business teachers and researchers play a significant role.
- "Business and society" courses will grow in number, but they must also grow in intellectual rigor.
- Greater sophistication is required in preparing and understanding the "social audits" that corporations are beginning to incorporate in their annual reports.

Courses in international business, pioneered as little as fifteen years ago in North America, will become more common. They may be constructed, however, on more rigorous prerequisites, including competency in speaking a foreign language, understanding another culture (through its literature, history, and religion), and periods of living, learning, and working in other lands.

While current courses focus on managing the multinational, new dimensions should be considered, which might include the following:

- *Comparative Commercial Law* — for nonlawyers;
- *Comparative Codes of Professional Conduct* — accounting, law, advertising, public relations in different countries;
- *International Unions* — their leaders, their memberships, their goals;
- *International Economic Organizations* — the European Economic Community, the International Monetary Fund, the Organization of Petroleum Exporting Countries, as well as other associations (e.g., the International Energy Agency) established to confront sudden problems;
- *Comparative Management Education programs* — including similarities and differences, graduates' performances, and the like, the purpose being to prepare managers to know the human resource base in a given region;
- *Transfers of Technologies* — especially in relation to Third World countries;
- *Foreign Markets* — as affected by demographics, government attitudes, consumer preferences;
- *International Accounting Standards and Practices* — an obvious need since accounting is the universal language of business;
- *Introduction of an international dimension into existing functional courses* — needed, because of the importance of international affairs in today's world, in such courses as marketing, accounting, finance, and business policy designed for managers in the domestic economy.

While the acquisition of skills in foreign language and developed competencies in understanding foreign cultures will enhance the attractiveness of students to multinationals, the demand-pull from such corporations will come only *after* the value of such studies has already been demonstrated. Opinions vary as to whether the university or the multinational corporation is more likely to provide leadership for this effort.

In conclusion, two dangers exist in regard to the life-long learning process. The first rests in the fact that "life-long learning" can become a fashionable cliché unless given substance by educators working in cooperation with business and government executives. The second danger related to noncognitive learning is its ambiguity and the need for sharper definitions of its content. Given these pitfalls, we could nevertheless lose great momentum if we fail to move aggressively with both research and teaching experiments in this field. If we are all on a learning path, if we are in the broad band of a continuum of learning, then life-long learning becomes a meaningful phrase and not a pious hope. If we are focusing primarily on the student at the beginning of the learning path, we need no longer feel that we must put everything into the curriculum that a student will need to know cognitively for the next twenty to thirty years. But we do need, at every stage of the learning path, at every stage of the learning continuum, to make sure that students and managers are learning to learn, that they are capable of analyzing their experiences, decisions, and actions so that they can continue the learning process for themselves and their organizations.

CHAPTER 17

Institutional Responses: Programs for Action

BORIS YAVITZ

Cross-cultural analyses tend to confirm that a crisis in higher education exists and that the crisis is global. Faculties have failed to distinguish between autonomy and accountability, to clarify the relationship between pure and applied research, and to establish professor-student interaction on a structured basis. Although the knowledge explosion spawns new disciplines and subdisciplines, their incorporation into curricula proceeds slowly; resolution of the fragmentation versus unity question is ineffectively addressed; older tenured professors are often perceived as roadblocks to entry

---

This chapter was written by Clarence C. Walton on the basis of an oral presentation by Boris Yavitz.

169

by young professors — even though the relationship between age
and creativity has never been satisfactorily demonstrated; "unionism" stirs emotions and breeds bitterness.

Particularly poignant is the story of Professor Bruno Zevi, who,
after thirty years' teaching at Rome University, resigned as professor
of architecture on the grounds that overcrowding, lack of contact
between student and professor, hostility toward scholarship, and
political partisanship had destroyed the university. There is a fear
that other "Zevi affairs" will occur in other countries.

Despite institutionwide constraints occasioned by tight budgets, spiraling costs, and prospective enrollment declines in some
countries, and, further, despite the lack of resolution of festering
academic problems, it is patent that management schools and institutes must ready themselves for novel and urgent problems in
regard to faculties, students, curricula, extra- and interinstitutional
arrangements, and life-long learning.

Faculties

Twenty years ago, when U.S. schools of business occupied a preeminent position in the higher education of managers, an awareness
grew that old modes of course content, intellectual profiles of what
constituted the acceptable faculty, and levels of education largely
restricted to the undergraduate had to be changed. Behind that perception was a realization that the basic contours of society and of
the corporation were changing so rapidly that old programs and old
slogans were obsolete. From those initial perceptions came new
courses, new faculty profiles, and new teaching devices that irre-
versibly altered the nature of business education in the United
States.

Today, too, a new sense is felt — but with a difference. The
awareness is well-nigh universal; the academic changes promise to
be more profound; the determination to respond is deep; the partnership for reform is more among equals; the challenges are global;
the value changes are pervasive; the learning process is broader as
life-long learning and noncognitive learning move into the educator's lexicon; the students are differently motivated. In short, the
perils of nonaction and ineffective response are great, even as the
promises of fulfillment through wise decisions, effectively implemented, are rich.

In light of the foregoing, faculties will be called upon to address the issues affecting their composition and effectiveness, their research orientations and their vision, their delivery systems, their promotion and tenure policies, and, finally, their own professional growth. Several conclusions flow from this premise.

Faculty composition will change perceptibly to include graduates from management and other schools and other talented and experienced individuals who do not hold traditional degrees.

This change in faculty composition will occur because fundamental changes in the learning process and in the learning continuum require cooperative arrangements with business organizations whose purpose historically has been restricted to the production of goods and services. From such organizations will come experienced people who may (1) serve on either a full- or part-time basis as clinical professors, (2) act on advisory boards, (3) cooperate in research, and (4) contribute to both curriculum and course innovations. The present "second-class" citizenship for those individuals will end.

Teaching effectiveness will be determined by new norms being superimposed on traditional criteria.

This change will involve the following two consequences:

- Faculties will assess their teaching effectiveness more by "outcome criteria" (achievement of graduates) and less by traditional grading of students.
- Considerable research will be devoted to discovering and validating new criteria for teaching performance, and educators are likely to undergo a decade of uncertainty.

A well-balanced faculty will accommodate its research orientations to include both pure and applied research and will sharply modify the different reward systems attached to effort in one type over another. It will be recognized that all research in schools of management is oriented toward those functions and obligations incumbent on all managers and on the staffs who support them.

The following two related observations are important:

- Applied research will frequently involve direct observation of the decision-making process *before* corporate policy is articulated.
- To test the validity of findings from pure and applied analyses, "bridges" between the two types of research will be needed.

A more imaginative use must be made of team teaching, which in concept and in practice will require a more fully integrated approach.

The team must be constantly with the class, must regularly share in developing the course, and must take cooperative responsibility for such items as syllabuses, grading, and examinations. The team must operate as a unity rather than a collectivity.

Management educators who have derived their organization and management theories from reference points in a North Atlantic culture must break from this rich yet constraining shell to open their visions to an understanding of other cultures and their meanings for theory.

Two momentous implications are contained in this proposition:

- The culture that Western managers have embraced, already fragile, will be further threatened.
- The search for the threads common to our humanity must intensify if cultural pluralism is not to degenerate into cultural anarchy.

Movements of faculty into business and of business executives into faculties on programmed and coordinated bases will become a recognized path to greater effectiveness and hence to career advancement.

- Programs akin to those now operating in New Zealand, France, Canada, Australia, and the United Kingdom will be expanded and, in some cases, made a factor in promotion policies.
- Dangers of haphazard movements by professors and practitioners must be minimized by careful selection processes and tailored learning programs.

Ways must be found to induce faculties to blend teaching, research, scholarship, and real-world experience in a "portfolio of abilities" that the school as a whole, if not the individual faculty member, must be able to deliver.

Students

Because of the employer's shifting needs and because of personal preferences, 1980 graduates will commonly have a two-career pattern by the year 2000 and will be anticipating a third. Career planning will take on a special meaning, and, partly as a consequence, recruiting patterns and admission criteria will be altered.

The following propositions derive from this prediction:

- Given the changing needs of changing individuals, institutions of higher learning and business organizations must pay greater attention to career planning. Just as corporations are developing sophisticated environmental scanning techniques, so, too, must they develop techniques for human resources scanning. Helping individuals to achieve higher levels of performance and a willingness to let such individuals enter multiple career paths (even outside the organization and with corporate help) will become essential to corporate strategy. Managers need to be taught to meet the employee's expectations. Unlike the career planning of the past, which was oriented to growth in jobs, the new planning will be oriented to development of the individual.

- Of paramount consideration in fostering career development are ways to combine the "worker-mobility" ideal of the West with the "worker-stability" preference of the East; to synthesize individual and group satisfaction; to relate short-term employment to lifetime employment by fusing rapid promotion to slow promotion processes; and to offer specialized career-path planning to nonspecialized personnel.

- Changing demographics and changing values suggest that career planning will include such novel features as the employment of husband and wife in one job with flexible adjustments to the needs of each; planning for double careers; involvement of children in the planning process to prevent serious dislocations to family life and to stress the importance of career planning to their own futures; the introduction of materials designed to teach for "unplanned" events, such as unexpected family break-ups, illnesses, plant closings, and dismissals; and the development of a new professional group within the corporate structure composed of career planning specialists who contribute to strategic and tactical planning.

To identify, recruit, and admit students who demonstrate potential for management, institutions will have to develop new batteries of tests and carry out more extensive prescreening and interviewing.

- Admission will be followed by opportunities in participative research, in which the student will be an apprentice to the master and will receive appropriate recognition for his or her contributions.
- Deliberate experimentation will be undertaken to provide an appropriate "student mix" — defined as a class composed of students oriented toward careers in nonprofit, public, and private profit organizations.

Curricula

Preparation of both generalists and specialists and the granting of degrees to those who complete the preparatory programs will continue in management schools. Traditional subjects will also continue to hold an important place in the management curriculum; a report submitted to the AACSB by a committee chaired by Dean H. J. Zoffer of the University of Pittsburgh provides a sound rationale for this conclusion. The Zoffer committee had discovered a virtual unanimity among American deans that accounting, economics, finance, marketing, production, the business environment, management, quantitative analysis, and operations research are among the major subjects that a quality institution must provide.

In addition to providing the basic functional courses, management education must pay increasing attention to the international dimension and to noncognitive skills. To educate both specialists and generalists, to synthesize both analytical and meta-analytical approaches to management theory, to enrich their own societies while cooperating with others, management institutions will be under constant pressure to be more innovative with their programs.

Some innovations could take the following forms:

- *Art of Negotiation.* Since the future will be shaped by "negotiated" arrangements in a transformed social contract, effective management requires education for effective negotiation. Teaching models should distinguish among (1) the "diplomatic" model, in which emphasis is on victory for enterprise (its inspiration comes from an old definition of a diplomat as a gentleman who is paid to lie persuasively on behalf of his country); (2) the "scientific" model, which, on the premise that "facts" speak for themselves, stresses hardheaded analysis and objective presentation of the findings; and (3) the "advocate" model, which relies on persuasion through careful marshaling of facts and selected emphases on those most conducive to one's cause.

- *Organization Theory.* Courses in this field will be expanded to include administration of (1) organizations dominated by professionals (e.g., accounting, insurance, and law firms), (2) cottage-industry "enterprises," (3) service and nonprofit enterprises, and (4) the "business" of government regulations.

- *Corporate Constitutionalism.* Growing resistance to the "firing" power of managers (embedded particularly in Western legal traditions and legitimized on the basis of ownership), rights of employees who disclose company malfeasance, and the presence of a philosophy of "social entitlements" may induce managers to consider such concepts as due process in industrial relations. Furthermore, "multiple-career" orientations will make it more important for corporations to provide inducements and protections to individuals in order to maintain a quality work force. If employers do not provide informal but effective safeguards, workers will become more litigious and will resort to the courts. Students require deeper grounding in political and constitutional theory.

- *Corporate Governance.* Western Europe has pioneered in efforts to restructure boards of directors to permit constituency representation, to encourage participative management, and to expand the concept of social responsibility. Given the pressures arising from internationalism, these efforts must be analyzed for their effectiveness, for their impact on board structures and managers, and for their applicability in other nations.

- *Environment Scanning.* It has already been noted that international competition, extension of the regulatory impact, and changing societal expectations are forcing managers to give more attention to "environmental-scanning" programs on issues once deemed unessential to the bottom line.

- *Internationalism.* International concerns, principles, and attitudes will profoundly influence the content and organization of courses in international business. Note that in the previous chapter, specific mention was made of new or drastically revised courses in comparative commercial law, comparative analyses of professions, the role of international unionism, significant international economic organizations, and international accounting standards and practices.

Reserved for final comment is an arresting development toward "knowing."

The question turns on the meaning and importance of noncognitive learning. The term *noncognitive* is troublesome because of its ambiguous nature. Business faculties are challenged to give specificity and operational meaning to the thesis advanced by Alfred North Whitehead to the Harvard Business School in 1939. Observed Whitehead:

> Imagination is not to be divorced from the facts: it is a way of
> illuminating the facts. . . . The tragedy of the world is that
> those who are imaginative have but slight experience, and
> those who are experienced have feeble imaginations. . . .
> The way in which a university should function in the
> preparation for an intellectual career, such as modern
> business or one of the older professions, is by promoting the
> imaginative consideration of the various general principles
> underlying the career. Its students thus pass into their period
> of technical apprenticeship with their imaginations already
> practiced in connecting details with general principles. The
> routine then receives its meaning, and also illuminates the
> principles which give it that meaning. Hence, instead of a
> drudgery issuing in a blind rule of thumb, the properly
> trained man has some hope of obtaining an imagination
> disciplined by detailed facts and by necessary habits.

It is now necessary to develop a terminology for a philosophy of education that extends the analytical process into meta-analytical terms, stresses the differences between (and the relationship of) analytical and synthetic approaches, and recognizes the role of intellect and of imagination, intellect and will.

Meta-analytical inquiry would examine the *range* of intellectual interest and of social involvements of individuals, the nature of work motivation, the use of energy, the control of time, the establishment of self-goals, emotional stability, tolerance of other opinions, adaptability to change, resiliency under stress, and qualities of honesty and loyalty, integrity and commitment, creativity and innovation.

From the foregoing one might conclude that experimental courses should be tried in teaching creativity, in demonstrating how creativity can be turned into managerial innovation, and in showing how people with creative talent can be identified and encouraged.

- Steps toward exploring the meaning of creativity and innovation should be taken in cooperation with psychologists, writers, painters, business entrepreneurs, and other gifted people.
- The relationship of business to the arts will receive more attention.
- Because of interest in a holistic approach to organization theory, in the nature and needs of the total personality, and in diverse cultures, the manager requires a more comprehensive understanding of theories relating to liberty, justice, and truth and of how such concepts are translatable to the enterprise and the individual.
- Courses on business and managerial ethics will multiply.

Extrainstitutional and Interinstitutional Relationships

Because of multiple and interrelated socioeconomic and political changes, management education requires greater flexibility; flexibility, in turn, demands careful experimentation. Two difficulties become apparent in the process. First is the problem of knowing

*how soundly constructed new programs actually are; second is the
problem of knowing not only what is going on among institutions
but also what is actually being learned from curricular experiments.*

- *Quality control.* It is suggested that consideration be given to
  devising ways to improve governmental and voluntary programs
  designed to assess the quality of management institutions.
- *Accreditation.* In countries that employ peer review, emphasis
  will be placed on the institution's special mission, the quality
  of the programs, and the faculty's will and competence to im-
  plement them. While core requirements may continue, the new
  accreditation will be more open to experimentation and more
  likely to be concerned with results than with students' test
  scores and faculty publications.

*The value of international cooperation has been demonstrated
often, and it should be continued. An international exchange system for management education and development is needed.*

- Papers prepared by a particular faculty for its own development
  needs could be exchanged with faculties of other institutions.
  Other papers detailing (1) the evolution, progress, and future of
  new courses within existing curricula and (2) institutional analyses of their own *overall strength* could be exchanged if trustees,
  presidents, and faculties approved.
- An international exchange system for management education
  and development could have enormous national and international implications by serving as a deterrent to any decline of
  standards, by providing patterns for reorganization of management institutions, and, above all, by affording enriched vicarious
  experiences so that the mistakes of some may not be the mistakes of all.

Life-Long Learning

In the discussion of life-long education, it is usually assumed that
learning occurs (1) on the job, (2) through in-house corporate programs, and (3) through graduate management education either in
a freestanding institute or in schools embedded within a university

structure. On this last point, one must ask: Is it desirable for universities to absorb management centers? Or for management centers to be totally independent? Or would some alternative relationship be preferable? These questions may tax our ingenuity in the near future.

Admittedly, a continuum of learning requires a better articulation and integration of universities, management schools or institutes, and corporate education, as well as an orchestration of professors, line managers, and professional management trainers. Yet it is interesting that while talking about the year 2010, one often neglects to mention the electronic media as an integrator. Should this omission be corrected?

We are agreed that (1) there will be more varied and diverse (both personal and corporate) demands on education and on training systems as corporations and individuals pass through different life phases, and (2) interaction, now generally poor between corporations and institutes, should be improved. However, the right kind of interaction is not going to be sufficient or effective unless there is a clear articulation of this process. To achieve better articulation requires modifications and improvements of the system. The key question is: Where will the motive force for the interaction come from? The following are the only two basic choices:

- *Central planning.* Under this alternative, somebody in government or in some institution decides how the pieces are to be linked and legislates that it be done. Most would agree that the result would be something close to disaster.

- *Voluntary initiative.* Under this alternative, management schools and centers must be the key initiators in any change process that affects the system because (1) management education institutions have already taken a significant initiative whose fruits should not be wasted, and (2) management educators are the professionals charged with the responsibility of defining the intellectual content of management and then transmitting it. Therefore, the burden is on management education.

Conclusion

Two themes provide memorable concluding notes. First is the recognition that the changes in management and management education contemplated in this volume are truly momentous. Second, there will be no overnight miracles and no sudden transformations by the waving of a magic wand. There will be hard work pursued with determination and persistence and, above all, with a belief in the rightness of our cause.

What should be done? Our responses need to be two-pronged to take into account intra- and interconstituency levels. On the former level we have to explain and to preach in order to convince our faculties and our students that great intellectual opportunities await if we move in the direction in which the stream is flowing and that, conversely, there are sad prospects of stagnation and decline if we do not. If we do not modify, someone else will. On the interconstituency level, it is already obvious what can happen. Windsor Castle and Arden House, Oslo, Chicago, and Paris are more than names of places where international conferences of managers have been held. They may be landmarks for an intellectual future marked by new national/international, educator/practitioner cooperative ventures.

CHAPTER 18

Reflections

MAURICE A. SAIAS and CLARENCE C. WALTON

Reflections of Maurice A. Saias

Reflecting what might be described as the hardheaded practical approach, William Tavoulareas (chapter 14) revealed a restiveness over whether free enterprise will remain competitive. Both the competitive spirit and the competitive style are confronted by growing public regulations that unfortunately take a domestic rather than a world view, and a continuance of this parochial trend threatens the power of a free-enterprise economy generally and the power of U.S. business particularly. The U.S. Congress and the various administrative agencies focus, for understandable reasons, on their large domestic markets, but they seem insensitive to global concerns. Business managers, on the other hand, who must adapt constantly if their enterprises are to succeed and to prosper, do reveal such a sensitivity.

It should be indicated publicly — and as pointedly as possible — that many in Western Europe give entirely too much credence to the hypothesis that economic power in the United States is rapidly decreasing. Reading the European press is like reading a corporate obituary column announcing that America is ready to be buried. I suspect that many on the Continent are going too far and too fast and that the Americans, with their vast human and economic resources, will make the kind of comeback that has marked that nation ever since its emergence as a full industrial power. The practical import for us educators is that neglect of that area of the world could impair vision of both the theory and philosophy of management.

Jacques Chaban-Delmas typifies a certain kind of outstandingly elegant European politician. His message (chapter 13) is urbane, polished, and distinguished, but the really interesting fact is that he struck the same note as Mr. Tavoulareas by stressing the necessity for business to remain competitive if it is to serve the needs of society. The assignment is to wed that spirit of competition to a respect for the freedom and dignity of individuals. In summary, therefore, the challenges are clear enough: to remain competitive, to remain free, and to remain civilized. In this threefold effort, educational leaders have an indispensable role to play.

Like Mr. Tavoulareas's message, the Chaban-Delmas message has practical import for management educators: In developing our courses, management faculties must constantly be aware of the fragile yet indispensable link between free political institutions and free economic institutions. In this awareness are seeds for an institutional philosophy of education. Since there is a growing rift between the market and the body politic, with the linkage being broken in some countries, it is clear that the contemporary world is in a crisis that is not temporary but that reflects a complex set of interrelated and profound changes. Because of this fact, it is impossible to build a totally reliable scenario for the future; actually, we face a set of multiple futures in which contingency planning may become just as important as the normal five-year plans that large corporations regularly undertake.

PURPOSES

In this brief summation, I would like to call your attention to four elements: the psychology of managers and management educators, perceptions of the environment, the "traps" to be avoided, and a chart of progress to date.

Psychology of Managers and Management Educators

Proceeding from the premise that society is moving through a pervasive and enduring revolution influenced by economic, technological, sociopolitical, and cultural factors, it is clear that we confront threats as well as opportunities. This dichotomy presents dangers. The presence of threat can paralyze action and limit vision. The potential of opportunities can spur greed and improvised decision-making. The role of today's managers and the role of tomorrow's managers are the same as the role of past managers — namely, to take the threat, make it a problem, and transform the problem into opportunity. For much too long we have been doing the opposite both in our companies and in our universities. Perhaps this is the most fundamental reason why we expect so much trouble in the years to come. My plea is for more hope and less fear, more confidence and less diffidence. It is much too early to assess the impact of our efforts, but if we embark on a course marked by trust in human capacities, our efforts will, on this account alone, become a milestone in the history of education.

Perceptions of the Environment

The conviction that rapid communications and common needs are shrinking the globe induces a heightened consciousness of the extranational environment. From such a backdrop come common sets of problems that force managers and educators to deal with the economic and political map of the world; with the relationships between industrialized nations and industrializing ones and between the developed/developing economies and the underdeveloped ones; with worldwide inflation and stagflation; and, finally, with the evolutionary pattern of technology. This global environment confronts both corporations and management faculties and partakes of certain commmon qualities.

It also should be remembered, however, that we confront issues posed within a specific context and through a specific environment and that these contexts and these environments differ from one country to another, from one sector to another. There is nothing new or startling in the observation that problems differ sharply from one industry to another, from one university to another, from one company to another. Possibly we are, at a minimum, moving to provide students with a better understanding of the global environment than with the more specific one with which they must deal. The reality is that a specific domestic, political, and regional environment provides the milieu in which managers must operate and professors must teach. In all honesty, I cannot foresee smashing success from our efforts to achieve educational reform if the focus is exclusively — even primarily — on the far distant, far removed, far diverse horizons and not on the near, the present, the discernible. Keeping our own commercial houses in order is paramount, and educating managers to serve as the "housekeepers" is our prime responsibility. If my perceptions are correct, it follows that management schools must recruit faculties who have a special interest and competence in domestic issues *and* in international issues. Not all faculty members will share concerns over the global nature of our problems, but such individuals should not, as a consequence, be denied access to our ranks.

Lest my message be misunderstood, a repetition is important. In no sense do I denigrate the importance of educating students about the international and global contexts within which the large corporations operate. Rather, I am suggesting that in our enthusiasm for this kind of education we should not neglect those things closer to home and, in many cases, closer to the hearts of our students.

The Traps

As management educators gear up to meet the challenges posed by a changing environment, they face the same problems that business executives face, and an incautious approach could land them in two traps. These might be described as the "time trap" and the "dichotomy trap." The former is found in the dilemma created by the obligation to develop proper capacities and to make appropriate preparations for the future. To develop such capacities too early is to waste resources. That waste, in turn, represents a cost that leads to decreased effectiveness and decreased stability for the community. On the other hand, not to develop timely resources to meet demands jeopardizes the very survival of the organization. Obviously, we are dealing here with the proactive and reactive stances that executives may take and that schools of management may take and teach. Very often the relationship between the proactive and reactive is misunderstood; very often the sense of proper timing is not inculcated; very often it is assumed that "getting the jump" on competitors guarantees success; very often a follow-the-leader stance is presumed to minimize risk. A time trap awaits all of us, and the trick is to recognize when we are sliding into the trap and to have appropriate "rescue" strategies available.

I have made reference also to the "dichotomy trap," which is found in the tendency to place issues in an either/or position. By so doing, various needs are placed in an unnecessarily adversarial mold. Examples come quickly to mind. They include corporate needs versus individual needs, internal demands versus external demands, diversity versus commonality, generalist versus specialist, cognitive versus noncognitive, issue-oriented versus discipline-oriented, teaching versus research, and in-house education versus outside education.

For much too long we have found it intellectually convenient to develop analytical models on the "versus" form. Dialectical reasoning is important, and much instruction can be garnered from the Hegelian approach to knowledge. It is my conviction, however, that the dialectic is only one part of the reasoning process and that synthesizing is equally important because it recognizes mutuality of needs, of possibilities, and of opportunities.

Charting Our Progress

Taking a backward glance clearly reveals that we educators have come a long way from those early days when persons — relatively unknown to one another — began to gather to ask a series of questions: Is a massive effort needed by management educators to position themselves to meet the future? Is a large-scale meeting on that topic practical? Would its results be meaningful? Obviously, no documentation is needed to indicate that these questions have been answered quite affirmatively. Yet much more needs to be done. Table 18.1 illustrates where we stand in this complex problem-solving journey.

The papers in this volume point toward major changes in business and society by the year 2000. The perception-information search for the project (i.e., phases A, B, and C in table 18.1) has thus

Table 18.1 Project Status

	Strategic	Administrative	Operational
Perception			
Information	A	B	C
Selection Choice	D	E	F
Implementation	G	H	I
Control		K	L

been successfully covered. We have clearly stated what ought to be done to meet new challenges (i.e., steps D and E indicate what it would take to do it, and suggestions have been made for Step F, curriculum redesign). The journey from A to F is a substantial one, and yet the table reveals the incomplete part of our agenda. As we prepare to move from G to L, it might be appropriate to say that we should not try to bring simple answers to complex problems. Let us not feel a necessity to destroy in order to build. Let us be not rigid but flexible. A phrase introduced by Boris Yavitz merits emphasis: Let us move to develop a "diversified portfolio of competencies." Further investments of time, energy, and money are required.

Reflections of Clarence C. Walton

We have struggled, with uneven success, to read the changing lines on Clio's face, recognizing fully that to speak of her in a future tense is to invite a certain contradiction. Nevertheless, it is our hope that by these efforts we may help Clio write a happier scroll for coming generations than that which unfolded throughout much of this twentieth century. We are all actors in a moving academic drama and, as in all great enterprises, first steps must be taken. They are reflected in this volume.

I should like to delineate briefly my sense of the significant advances we have made — and what they portend — by striking out in two directions: (1) to identify certain implications that have not surfaced in clear and palpable form in these papers and (2) to place this material within a context that addresses both the mood and the reality of our times.

SIGNIFICANT IMPLICATIONS

To convey my perceptions of certain implications that follow from the preceding papers, I propose to examine what was said about curriculum and faculty.

Curriculum

To confront the problems related to curriculum is to be chastened immediately by the certain knowledge that course reform has been likened frequently — and accurately — to projects for relocating cemeteries. Emotions intensify; positions harden; fears deepen; vested interests surface. Within such an emotional context there is room for the cynicism expressed by those who believe firmly that the birth of every new curriculum is somehow the product of people long dead. Relevant is the observation of Margaret Mead, the late distinguished American anthropologist, that every academic innovation is, at the moment of its implementation, totally obsolete because individuals learn of things and events not covered in classrooms. They learn through a variety of instrumentalities: media, theatre, dance, peer influences, churches, social clubs, and the like. These teaching — or quasi-teaching — media are neither fully shaped nor controlled by the learned societies and communities of which we are a part. Nonetheless, educators play a critical role, and what has been said about the need for curriculum reform is important. A few illustrations demonstrate the main point.

There has been expressed a concern over the distinction and relationship between entrepreneurship and creativity. Obviously, in handling the concept of creativity, business professors have much to learn from other creative people — painters, poets, architects, choreographers, and novelists. Douglas P. Hofstadter's book, *Goedel, Escher and Bach*, provides an instructive lesson. Hofstadter recalls the great dream of Alfred North Whitehead, Bertrand Russell, and others to make mathematics the queen of all sciences. From this "monarch" of numbers and equations would come the logic for all sciences and all scientific propositions. In the domain of business the computer would reign supreme. But the human animal behaved — in roles as manager, employee, supplier, and consumer — in ways that made us quickly realize that the computer "brains" were limited. Hofstadter, dispersing multiple clues to show why mathematical applications are limited, uses the brilliant Austrian mathematician Goedel to serve as an intellectual devil's advocate.

Identifying basic weaknesses in the assumptions of Whitehead and Russell in his own masterwork, *Principia Mathematica*, Goedel demonstrated, mathematically, why mathematics could not explain all. Hofstadter, accepting Goedel's conclusions that the computer could never replicate the human mind, went on to ask the important question: What is in the human intellect that makes it so distinctive? So nonduplicative? To answer his own question, Hofstadter turned from the mathematician to creative artists like Escher and Bach. Deeply conscious of our debt to mathematics, business scholars recognize their need for help from other sources.

What this volume has done is to bring forth the "Hofstadter" latent in all of us by stressing the need for creativity in curriculum revision and by emphasizing what is known but sometimes forgotten — namely, that creativity is fostered through cooperation with other faculties. If engineering, law, psychology, and mathematics helped in the past, the humanities may be of special help in the future, when management faculties will more fully emphasize creativity and entrepreneurship, communications and interpersonal relationships, bargaining and negotiating skills, administration and leadership.

Because the humanities have historically addressed issues now identified as important to the formation of a manager, it is singularly important that in seeking to clear the theoretical underbrush, we consult with our colleagues in history, philosophy, theology, and literature. Their experiences may serve us well. However, in that consultation the selection process must be very sophisticated because humanists — sad to say — have themselves become addicted to narrow specializations. The net result is that the very things that should most concern them — humanity's struggles, goals, and ambitions — have sometimes been subordinated to analytical discourses on small fragments of the human personality or on methodological problems.

If getting the "right" people from the humanities to help in this enterprise is important, so, too, is a related issue that is dormant but explosive. I refer to the philosophy of education that will inspire and permeate efforts by management faculties. To state the issue concretely, let us recall that the approach to humanistic education was predicated on the belief that reading and understanding the classics enabled free individuals to participate meaningfully in the democratic process. People needed to think and talk. People still need to think and talk. But in a society whose common values are in disarray, thinking and talking in a common vocabulary becomes difficult. Faculties are caught in a dilemma. To speak in many "tongues" risks creating a Babel; to speak in one tongue may produce an idiom that reflects the very parochialism they decry. Management schools face a formidable assignment in introducing the right mix of eclecticism and absolutism into their quest for a satisfactory philosophy of education. And a philosophy is needed to prevent aimless drifting or ill-conceived programs.

The strong emphasis given to the importance of noncognitive learning raises, at least in one specific case, a special danger. It is found important not to use the term as a grab bag for all those interests that are receiving inadequate attention within existing curricula. In this intellectual adventure — rather new to business faculties — the preliminary spadework must go long and deep.

To complete this summation, let us recall a sobering fact: In textbooks written some thirty years ago, there was no talk of computers, of inflation accounting, of multinationals, of decision theory, and the like. The point established is a chastening one. It is a reminder that, for all our efforts, there will be developments we have not anticipated — and possibly should have. Such developments will undoubtedly have a significant impact on business and on management teaching. On the other hand, if there is any wisdom in the cliché that "two heads are better than one," then there is hope that we, as a collectivity of experienced people, will do a better job than our predecessors.

Faculty

A theme iterated and reiterated in these papers is that partnerships between the university and the corporation must intensify. Explicit mention was made of the need to involve executives in both teaching and research as well as in service on advisory councils; such involvement should not be used simply as a facade for fund-raising purposes. The cautionary note is well taken: Busy executives will not commit themselves if their contributions are not taken seriously. This means that before exchange programs are launched, faculties must define precisely the role they are willing to accord to business executives, the incentives they will provide, and the weight they will give to practitioners' opinions. This is especially important in view of the long history of tension between academics and business executives.

When faculty takes the initiative, it is clear that the professoriate itself must come to a collective judgment on what it expects from the "outsiders," the "price" of the partnership, and the institutional means whereby "outsiders" can be incorporated into the institutional fabric. It is unlikely that professors will dissent from this proposition. It is less likely that they will take early steps to bring the partnership into existence and to discipline themselves to the sacrifices that every marriage entails.

A further warning might be issued. As the business faculty responds to challenges to teach leadership, to revise organization theory, to take a holistic approach, to accommodate itself to international pressures, and to weave multiple strands from other disciplines into its theorizing, there is a danger that it might be viewed by others as embarking on a form of academic imperialism. If this ever becomes the perception of other faculties, then we had better prepare well for the fight we are inviting. Other faculties, particularly in the humanities, are already tense because enrollments are declining, budgets are stabilizing, new programs are being discouraged, and existing ones are being criticized. Inflation ravages incomes; so does declining enrollment.

Aside from such practical concerns, there are other reasons for approaching the coming task with appropriate humility. Intellectual history is largely the story of a knowledge explosion that has bred different disciplines. Political philosophy shifted into social philosophy and then into political economy, which, in turn, divided into political science and economics. Psychology, economics, and engineering were used to lay the basis for management. Obviously, then, there are good reasons why new disciplines come into being. Even to hint that these academic walls, like those of Jericho, should come down is to stimulate questions of great importance to our own enterprise. Who built these academic walls? Why? Which ones should come down? Who are the builders for the future?

Since there is obviously a shift of enormous magnitude in the goals of business organizations — from exclusive concern with the bottom line to concern with things beyond the bottom line — it follows that meta-economic issues become more important to managers and to management theory. If management faculties take postulates from other disciples too indiscriminately, they may inadvertently weaken the conceptual pillars of other fields. On the other hand, if business faculties borrow — and return — they can have an invigorating influence on all education. My plea is for the development of strategies that will enrich the totality of higher education. What we have embarked upon is therefore substantially different from reform efforts mounted on previous occasions. Awareness of these subtleties must be deepened.

MOOD AND REALITY: TOWER AND SPIRE

The social landscape seems littered with the wreckage of old symbols and old dreams. Pessimism abounds. The report of a significant meeting of European business leaders at Davos in February 1980 indicated that their perceptions were characterized by large doses of unmitigated gloom. Other analysts, seeking to describe a frightening rise in terrorism, use such terms as *Eurofacism* and *Euromarxism*. Vietnam and Afghanistan still loom as ugly scars on the face of the globe; suspicions of "superpowerism" by small nations are matched by concerns among large states over possible adventurism by the smaller states.

There is, on the other hand, a profound sense that great problems make for great opportunities. A European Parliament, the first such elected body in contemporary history, has just come into being. Viewed with either great hope or great cynicism, that parliament nonetheless suggests a coming of new institutional forms to meet unprecedented problems. If its vision of the future is reasonably accurate, management education also requires certain new formats. We shall define the future and we shall develop the vision by asking ourselves some simple questions. While the questions could take a variety of forms, everyone must ultimately ask these two:

What is the source of my intellectual inspiration?

What is the source of my spiritual inspiration?

To answer the first question leads to a recognition that Alfred North Whitehead's maxim regarding the life of learning has great importance for us: Knowledge and action are inseparable. Never to be forgotten is the fact that an essential ingredient of managerial education is the ultimate testing of knowledge in application.

Whitehead was relevant to business scholars before. He is relevant
now. He will be relevant in the future.

Related to the second question is the following: How do we
perceive the relationship of intellect to will, reason to appetite, the
pragmatic to the normative? We have used *noncognitive* as a term
to capture reasons why these relationships must be honored and
understood. Perhaps symbolism will help when debates are forgotten, words misunderstood, and generalizations challenged. Paris,
where the final conference on which this volume is based took
place, has these symbols. By staying in our minds, they will inspire
fatiguing wills toward continuing efforts. For example, look hard
at the Cathedral of Notre Dame and at the Eiffel Tower. The first
took nearly 182 years to build; the second was completed in eight
months. Roland Barthes lovingly described the latter "as a place
where one can dream, observe, understand, marvel, shop — cut off
from the world and yet owner of the world." Eiffel is, above all,
symbol.

The cathedral, too, is symbol. Looking at those glorious landmarks of this exciting city, recall with me one story told at the
dedication of the Eiffel Tower in 1889 by a reporter whose impres-
sionistic piece, now paraphrased, was this:

> I watched a full moon drifting through a clouded sky. As the
> fireworks exploded to dramatize the dedication of the Eiffel
> Tower, as people cheered this fascinating engineering
> achievement even as critics poured scorn, the moon came
> from behind a cloud to light the spires of Notre Dame.
> Looking upward at both I mused on this important question:
> will my beloved France have a future which recognizes —
> and reconciles — the meaning of the Spire and the meaning
> of the Tower?

That question still haunts us, and it is important to recognize that
any present disarray will not be repaired without knowledge of facts
and sensitivity to symbols. Insights have poured forth in abundance
in this volume. Symbols have already been created for us. In conclusion, might we close our eyes to open our minds — and thus
remember symbols as we review challenges. We have a historic
opportunity to continue a peaceful enterprise — to educate wisely
and well those who will manage the critical institutions of our
worlds. By working with people, for people, and by people, we may
come to merit the description once applied by the French to their
Black Robes of the New World: a *force civilatrice*.

CHAPTER 19

Highlights of Part III

ROBERT H. B. WADE

Background and Environment

- Western European managers and schools of management have achieved a degree of maturity that has moved them from a position second to that of the United States to one of full and equal partnership; on the other hand, since the Third World is likely to be a powerful force in the coming decades, more attention must be paid to it.

- Socioeconomic changes will become so complex and take place so rapidly that students now attracted to business because of its perceived stability may be reluctant to pursue careers in it. Because a new and different type of student may be attracted to management, recruiting as well as measurement and testing techniques may require significant modification.

- In the development of effective managers, work experience and life-long education will be seen increasingly as an integrated whole.

Educational Mission

- Better articulation between management schools or institutes and corporations is required, as is better orchestration of academics, professional developers, and line managers.
- Diversity in approach and mission of schools of management should be encouraged by flexible structures and guidelines; it should not be hampered by overly rigid criteria.

Life-Long Learning

- The concept of life-long learning will spread. The "front-end load model" of education is already obsolescent, since management schools cannot teach everything the future manager needs to know.
- Because career planning requires greater attention than ever before, institutions of learning *and* of business will become partners, deeply involved with individuals in their career planning and development.
- Human resources training and development are an integral part of corporate strategic planning and cannot be relegated to a place of lesser importance. The enterprise itself is a growing resource for in-house training in ways that accomplish corporate and individual goals through the training process.
- Management schools and institutes will increasingly respond to the needs of individuals contemplating second and third careers as well as to the special problems posed by the dual career paths of husband and wife.

Curriculum

- Students must be educated as specialists *and* generalists, not exclusively as one or the other.

- Since noncognitive skills (e.g., communication, interpersonal, and negotiating skills) are essential to managerial effectiveness, development of such skills should be included in the curriculum, but not at the expense of technical or cognitive knowledge.
- Development of noncognitive skills should be integrated as much as possible into the existing curriculum in order to establish a base for life-long learning, referred to by the conference as a "continuum of learning" or the "learning path."
- The business environment and public policy dimension of the management curriculum needs additional emphasis, including appreciation of management tasks in both public and private sectors.
- Since the international dimension of business is increasing, the international dimension of the curriculum must increase correspondingly.
- Management schools and institutes must develop analytical approaches to courses in managerial and business ethics and to the impact of differing societal expectations on basic values.

Faculty

- Ways must be found to induce faculties to blend teaching, research, scholarship, and real-world experience in a "portfolio of abilities" that management faculties as a whole — if not their individual members — must be able to deliver.
- There should be less resistance by business professors to "team teaching" and "team research" involving other disciplines, such as psychology, philosophy, ethics, law, and political science.
- Practitioners should be welcomed as fully participating partners in course and curriclm development.

Research

- A better balance should be struck between basic and applied research. Emphasis on action-oriented, issue-oriented research is needed in areas like entrepreneurship, creativity, and innovation, in social trends, on the changing nature of work and the work ethic, and on organizational adaptability and research.

Toward Implementation

- A worldwide network to provide exchanges of information among business schools is of paramount importance.
- The efforts on which this volume is based are but the first of many steps toward more enduring and more substantial cooperation among faculties and managers throughout the world.

Epilogue: Retrospects and Prospects

CLARENCE C. WALTON

There is little doubt that the future is a chiaroscuro whose lights and shadows dance intermittently before us. Although it is impossible to predict precisely what is going to happen, it is nevertheless possible to predict precisely what *should* happen. In general terms the message is this: If the future requires more enlightened leadership, institutions and firms must move into a closer partnership to produce more enlightened leaders. There cannot be better businesses without better managers, better parliaments without better parliamentarians, better schools without better faculties. The issue is as simple — and as complex — as that. The overall challenge is reducible to two words: *more* and *better*.

To achieve this overall goal requires a measure of intellectual breadth that permits effective leadership to operate within a milieu where competing theories struggle for ascendancy and where constructive reasoning is not subordinated to the destructive reasoning so common to our past learning patterns. Perhaps much can be learned about such a milieu from the history of Western Europe. Since the days of Bismarck, Western Europe has learned to live with two almost contradictory streams of influence. On one hand, there was the socialist labor movement, which advocated democracy in both the industrial and political spheres and which agitated for a more active role in the formation of national and corporate policies. Against this stream was a formal and extensive web of financial controls in which competition was seen as the discipline most required to promote the public good and national autonomy.

Perhaps what we face today is a challenge to combine a series of antitheses into a dialectic that, if unable to achieve a final theoretical synthesis, allows people of diverse ideologies, different nationalities, competing economic systems, and different cultural commitments to live in peace and prosperity. The radical skepticism of the Montaignes of our world, which has provided the dominant motif for universities, must be modified by, or at least joined to, a more constructive philosophy of education.

This herculean effort to develop a synthesis on which is built a more commodious edifice of management theory can succeed only if the professional side of education impacts positively the liberal side of education. The whole thrust of liberal learning, so salutary in its emphasis on critical reasoning, must now be counterbalanced by learning programs that stress constructive reasoning; in the presence of disintegrating features of contemporary society there is need to relate diverse parts into a meaningful whole. Criticism of a weak component in an otherwise sound system should be accompanied by suggestions to repair it.

As business scholars prepare for this historic assignment, it is well to remember that in the conferences from which this volume derives not all significant trends were identified, not all generalizations properly scrutinized, and not all reform suggestions thoroughly exposed. To do justice to those conference participants whose varied opinions may not have appeared in the various subgroup summaries, it was deemed useful to record as many of their opinions as possible. They constitute, in the aggregate, a useful backdrop against which the agendas for future meetings can be judged.

The Changing Work Force

Before the end of the century, industrialized nations will undergo a major change in the nature of their respective work forces. White male family breadwinners, typical of the past, will become a minority.

This cultural shift is even now revealed in the following developments:

- The idea of life-long motherhood roles and life-long labor roles, pillars of a gender-divided society, are falling — sometimes out of choice and sometimes because living costs force households to have two breadwinners.

- A great increase in "knowledge" jobs will prove so attractive to a growing percentage of highly educated women that the historic definition of "back-breaking" toil as requiring "male muscle" will diminish as a significant factor in work.

- The declining number of children within the typical family, coupled to community services that help in the upbringing of children, will insure greater worker involvement by women. (Childrearing as a profession may become characteristic of a new element in the work force.)

- The family may increasingly come to be regarded as a consumer buying unit, and households will consist of childless couples, groups of adults living together, single-parent families, and the like.

- Working couples will become so common that (1) "flexi-time" in work hours and (2) job descriptions allowing a couple to perform a single task for a single salary are probable.

- Workers, male and female, will intensify the egalitarian trend so that the Swedish pattern of a "solidaristic wage policy" (designed to narrow wage differentials between groups of workers) will likely spread. (Note: An important side effect of the Swedish commitment was expressed in a government report, prepared under Rudolph Meidner's chairmanship, which observed that increased productivity was essential if egalitarianism is to grow.)

- Power centers will be broken, and what Michael Crozier said of France may become true of all developed nations of the world: "The world of tomorrow makes it imperative that elites abandon

their monopolistic traditions, open the door to individual competition and collective cooperation, and willingly accept the rise
of people of lowly social origins."

- If managers fail to project moderate adjustments in the power
  structure, others will step forward to promise more radical
  changes. The clash between participative democracy and functional democracy (where officials responsible to various groups
  participate in national decisions) may shape up as a major political issue.

- To use the words of Chris Argyris, workers in advanced countries will "obtain optimum personality expression while at work
  if provided with jobs which permit them to be more active than
  passive; more independent than dependent; to have longer
  rather than shorter time perspectives; to occupy higher positions
  than their peers; to have control over their world; and to express
  many of their deeper, more important abilities" (*Personality
  and Organizations: The Conflict between System and the Individual* [New York: Harper & Brothers, 1957], p. 53).

- The expansion of the "graying population," caused by increasing
  longevity, creates a demand for transfer payments (old-age
  health and income benefits), and the elderly's needs may clash
  with young workers' demands. An intergenerational conflict of
  unpredictable intensity may occur.

Population Movement: Urbanism versus Suburbanism

*Contrasting patterns of population concentrations between the
developing and developed nations are evident, and the manager's
role in meeting diverse human needs will become more complex.*

The patterning is illustrated by the following:

- Mass migrations in poorer countries from countryside to city
  are creating serious socioeconomic crises. China is working to
  halt the migratory tide into the cities by bringing health and
  education to the rural population and by establishing self-sufficient cooperatives and communes. Of India's population of
  600 million, over 120 million (20 percent) live in cities where
  housing conditions are desperate, unemployment extensive, and
  a twenty-four-hour clean water supply nonexistent. Mexico

City, Tokyo, Caracas, and Rio are symbols of what Arnold Toynbee saw as the major problem of the next century — namely, people living in an "ecumenopolis" or world city, where population density places great strains on all human services.

- Population will continue to rise and, again, more intensively in the less developed areas of the world. For example, the rate of population growth in Kenya is approaching a 3.5 percent increase per year — almost the highest in the world — and the country's problems are compounded by the lack of suitable farming land. What is true of Kenya is fairly typical of East Africa generally, where even wildlife reserves are in danger.

- Against this worldwide trend are the experiences of certain advanced industrialized countries where large cities are losing population. In the United States, for example, 60 percent of the people live on the outskirts of the major cities, and the migration, being a selective process, is leading to more extensive economic and social segregation. The average suburban family is younger, better educated, and richer than the family in the inner city. While problems differ between countries, they are severe everywhere. New York's financial crisis, for example, is symptomatic of larger concerns. The urban crisis may be compounded by, for example, the potentially divisive struggle currently emerging between an industrially active Northeast and a booming Southwest in the United States, or between England and a potentially oil-rich Scotland.

- Paralleling America's regional tensions are other nations' concerns over ethnic claims. Basques in Spain, Bretons in France, and Ukranians in Russia are illustrations of ethnic problems in many areas of the world. Recruiting, training, and rewarding new managers from such diverse groups will constitute a heavy assignment for business executives and public officials.

The New Technology

While the conventional wisdom holds that applications of technology will continue to increase at a quickening pace, the new technological world will possess a distinguishing characteristic: The new technology will not be restricted to specific applications (e.g., steampower in the nineteenth century and electricity in the twentieth) but will have widespread uses.

- The large-scale microminiaturized integrated units of the coming technological world have almost limitless applications. The scope of digital technology; the modest cost and size of the hardware; the economies of scale; the diversities of applications in standardized programs; the safety, speed, and flexibility of operations; and the lower energy needs that may develop all make present technology richer than what has preceded it. Microprocessing is already visible in automobile production, consumer goods, communications, and engineering processes, and to it will be joined developments in lasers and fiber optics in the field of medicine. Microbiology, microphotography, traffic control, retail distribution, and the like will be affected.

- The increased obsolescence of existing physical and human capital will tend to outrun programs for retraining and for business/labor adaptations in organizations, and this may slow the pace of change. However, the masses may become increasingly dissatisfied with political, economic, educational, or social impediments. Contemporary educational systems, attitudes toward work and leisure, techniques for financing reequipment, and social mechanisms for redistribution appear so inadequate that managers will experience greater public pressures for innovation. Labor is not homogeneous, and people take time to learn new skills. Progress must be viewed as a bank where, in today's terms, technical assets are running well ahead of withdrawals. The consistent failure to maintain full employment indicates a serious weakness.

- Intensified pressures on scarce capital for investment will occur because the increased costs for investment and technology are matched by rising costs for producing raw materials. Dr. Walter Caspar, a manager of Metallgesellschaft AG, was quoted as saying that Europeans are facing a "long period of noticeable increases of the specific costs of producing raw materials" and that the greater expenses were due to higher exploration costs and to greater distances from major traffic routes of some newly discovered deposits. The distances require enormous expenditures for the infrastructure — roads, housing, water supply, and the like. The European Economic Community has expressed much the same view as Dr. Caspar.

- While the specific nature of the new pressures is hard to delineate with precision, it is clear that when the ratio of labor to capital falls and the ratio of capital to output does not rise correspondingly, management will be challenged to remove the two main obstacles to the diffusion of new technology — lack of knowledge by managers themselves and public fears of mass unemployment. The area of industrial relations will be more broadly conceived by top executives.

Alterations in Economies

Some experts are thinking the unthinkable when they suggest that industrialized societies are approaching some sort of evolutionary cul-de-sac — that is, moving toward an "entropy state," which may be defined as a society where complexity and interdependency have reached such unmanageable proportions that they equal (or exceed) the society's productive capabilities.

Reasons for this dismal assessment include:

- The probability that "slumpflation" will intensify as rising inflation and rising unemployment go unchecked hand in hand.
- Prospects for different scenarios for both capitalism and socialism. Despite their intellectual antagonism, Marx and Keynes agreed on one thing: A decreasing rate of capital investment would ultimately lead to the demise of capitalism. From the socialist side are also heard strident cries of dissatisfaction that taxes and regulations have become oppressive. Public leaders will press the productive sectors — and their managers — to do more and more.
- The potential for intensified hostility toward business executives if they merge their organizations with others to achieve economies of scale.
- Threats of a breakup of large organizations. This alternative is made plausible by a sense that the successful business organization of the future will not produce standardized products or services for mass consumption, but customized products and services. Because customer products will depend on standardized components fitted together carefully, small production facilities are possible. There could be a return to the cottage

industries of two centuries ago, with whole families involved in the work, which would replace large, assembly-line factories. Instead of going to a central place to work, employees might work at home. Workers would own tools; clusters of entrepreneurs might make short- or long-term contracts with an organization. The management of such clusters will provide new opportunities for expanding management theory because "independent" producers and "invisible" planners challenge managerial resources. Coordinating these independents and motivating them will challenge managers in new organizational configurations.

Alteration in Business Organizations

Taken together, the forces outlined above make organizational restructuring and vigorous entrepreneurship high priorities for the coming decades. Whatever adjustments come, managers will be needed for organizations that differ in size, in function, in authority structures, and in manpower requirements.

Major considerations relate to the following:

- Given the need to preserve a balance among large, medium-size, and small firms, relevant training must be provided to their managers.

- In one critical service area, the office organization, dramatic changes are in store. Printed paper routines, which consume so much time, will vanish; mail sorting, letter opening, stamping, and file searching will decrease significantly as electronic forms and transmissions advance rapidly. The result will be a profound change in the social structure of the office. Workers may even seek excuses to come into contact with others. Managers at all levels will probably be forced into new behavioral modes of leadership and direction.

- A fresh dialectic is required to reconcile sharply different approaches to management. One working group at Paris, noting the movement from autocracy to democracy, from an aristocratic distemper to a democratic temper, concluded that restructuring will not be "driven by a single sprocket or by a single engine from a single center."

- Companies will be required to operate under carefully developed and precisely focused strategic plans. Providing strategic directions to the corporation is a responsibility that will fall on either board chairmen or chief executive officers. The strategist will constantly be evaluating and determining the markets that will be served, the competition to be met, and necessary adaptations through acquisition or divestitures. As noted, the risk of investing in new technology may increase, and the added dangers may cause managers to become too conservative.

Shifting Elite Relationships

There appears to be a fundamental shift in relationships between government and business elites and even between elites having no formal commitment to either the public or the private organization.

Some probable consequences of the shifts are:

- A closer partnership will develop between government and corporate leaders in certain projects. This development is reflected by growing interest in the theory propounded by N. D. Kondratieff: Investments come in "long moves of fifty-year swings from peak to peak." If the Kondratieff curve is correct, businessmen will work with public leaders in giving as much sedulous attention to the problems of supply as the Keynesians gave to problems of demand. The likely result is a form of cooperative planning not heretofore experienced by leading nations of the Western world.

- Both public and private administrators, sensing that the regulatory sector is itself "big business" that becomes counterproductive if not managed well, will have a common interest in promoting efficiency. Education for "regulatory" administrators is a necessity.

- Within even the traditional elites, tensions will be occasioned by different perceptions of the society's and the organization's basic needs — and of appropriate responses thereto.

- Of particular interest will be the intellectual elites that Joseph Schumpeter predicted would become powerful enough to bring down the house of capitalism.

- Finally, the knowledge explosion will give rise to new professions with their own codes, which may conflict with other professional codes inside the country and with codes of other countries. These professionals and paraprofessionals will exercise increasing power over both the public and the private bureaucracies because of their mastery of the information-gathering process and of the information itself and because of their ability to communicate with other specialists in other areas. In short, managers may face problems with professionals that will rival their historical problems with workers.

Internationalism's Future Face

The coming international order poses both great threats and great opportunities. If managers establish themselves in world opinion as committed to the exchange of goods rather than to an exchange of evils, to fulfillment of promises rather than to execution of threats, possibilities for peace and prosperity will be substantially enhanced.

Internationalism will continue to grow because:

- Economic dominance by any single nation is ending, as the 1979 report from the OECD documented.
- Revolutions in the technology of communication will bring diverse peoples into closer contact.
- The number of industrialized nations will increase. (From England almost alone in the eighteenth century, we moved to England, France, Germany, and the United States in the nineteenth century. Japan, Russia, Canada, and Brazil have been added in this century.) This ever-enlarging arc of sophisticated societies must be built on some core cooperation if peace is to be preserved.
- Shortages of critical, nonrenewable raw materials lead to greater interdependence. Industrial nations clearly recognize that until the energy constraint is lifted, growth and welfare may take the form of efforts to increase job satisfaction rather than wages for workers, more diverse rather than better products for consumers. Ad hoc adjustments by both governments and businesses will stretch leaders' ingenuity.
- While the awakening of hitherto sleeping giants in the Third

World creates opportunities for new resources and new markets, it also creates possibilities for dangerous rivalries. Third World countries are already in debt to commercial banks alone in excess of $300 billion; over the next two decades they need to create productive employment for a work force likely to expand by more than 500 million people. From different sources come warnings about North-South relationships. At the time of the Paris conference, Robert McNamara announced his coming retirement as president of the World Bank and took the occasion to call attention to the seriousness of the situation in which no industrial nation gives even 1 percent of its gross national product to development assistance. In addition, Willy Brandt, chairman of the Independent Commission on International Development Issues, reminded the world of a desperate necessity to see the "menacing long-term problems" — a world of poverty and hunger where resources are squandered without consideration of renewal, where more arms are made and sold than ever before, and where bombs tick.

- "Superpowerism" may come to be more suspect than ever before. More countries may seek to establish for themselves what Yasuhiro Nakasome, director general of the Japanese Self-Defense Agency, described as Japan's major policy: "to have long ears sensitive to sounds like the rabbit [and] the defensive power of the porcupine to ward off foreign bodies." The other side of the coin is the possibility of small-nation adventurism. The dangers are substantial, and managers will be caught in conflicting currents.

- As individual nations jockey for position in this competitive world, they will identify "critical industries" as essential to national survival, and this identification will be done by government leaders in cooperation with the business community in modes suggestive of mercantilism. However, the new mercantilism will differ from the old if the definition offered in a 1977 lecture by Edmund Dell, former secretary for trade in the British government, is correct: Mercantilism does not necessarily rule out free trade or require protection, but it does demand a calculation of what is in the country's best interest.

- While the view has been expressed that the great corporate dinosaurs called the transnationals would continue to dominate international trade, important shifts are even now occurring in international markets. For example, established banks are experiencing a leveling off of growth. The core of large corporations is generally tied to a domestic orientation.

The Future of Management Education

Because of the convergence of socioeconomic, political, and organizational forces on managers, those who educate them face problems of institutional restructuring, faculty training and retraining, and curricula planning on an unprecedented scale. In some countries institutional problems threaten to block effective responses.

Organization theory, broadly conceived, will be defined in terms appropriate to the diverse associations managers will be called upon to serve; motivation will be better understood as meta-analytical research efforts bear fruit; theories of leadership and distinctions between leader and bureaucrat will be sharpened; the coalescing of different kinds of teachers from the worlds of theory and of work will alter faculty membership; and the deliberate mixing of students in class patterns designed to further their appreciation of management in different undertakings may bring new understanding.

It is perhaps overly ambitious to link the efforts of the contributors to this volume to the efforts of medievalists in the eleventh century. During that period there was a shift away from emphasis on the individual in an oral culture to emphasis on the office emanating from written law. Struggling to adapt to the change, theorists began to fashion abstractions for authority, law, office, and freedoms; by so doing, they literally "invented" the state. The observations, ideas, and predictions gathered here may be the first big step toward "inventing" a new profile of managers — and of ways to educate them.

List of Volume
Contributors

DANIEL BELL, Professor, Department of Sociology, Harvard University, Cambridge, Massachusetts

FLETCHER BYROM, Chairman of the Board, Koppers Company, Inc., Pittsburgh, Pennsylvania

JACQUES CHABAN-DELMAS, Former Prime Minister of France, Former President of the French National Assembly

NEIL CHAMBERLAIN, Professor, Graduate School of Business, Columbia University, New York, New York

DAVID CHAMBERS, Faculty Dean, London Business School, London

MAX B.E. CLARKSON, Professor, Faculty of Management Studies, University of Toronto, Toronto, Ontario

WILLIAM R. DILL, President, Babson College, Babson Park, Massachusetts

BOHDAN HAWRYLYSHYN, Director, International Management Institute, Geneva

FRANS VAN DEN HOVEN, President, Unilever N.V., Rotterdam

JAMES ROBERTSON, Writer and Futurologist, Author of *The Sane Alternative*, Shropshire

IGNACY SACHS, Director, International Research Center on Environment and Development, Ecole des Hautes Etudes en Sciences Sociales, Paris

MAURICE A. SAIAS, Professor, Institut d'Administration des Entreprises, University of Aix-Marseille, Aix-en-Provence

WILLIAM P. TAVOULAREAS, President, Mobil Oil Corporation, New York, New York

JAN TINBERGEN, Nobel Laureate, Professor Emeritus, Erasmus University, Rotterdam

CLARENCE C. WALTON, Professor, The American College, Bryn Mawr, Pennsylvania

BORIS YAVITZ, Dean, Graduate School of Business, Columbia University, New York, New York